THE QUOTABLE MISES

MARK THORNTON, EDITOR

For information write the Ludwig von Mises Institute, 518
West Magnolia Avenue, Auburn, Alabama 36832; Mises.org

Large Print Edition published 2012 by Skyler J. Collins.
Visit: www.skylerjcollins.com

ISBN-13: 978-1479384990
ISBN-10: 1479384992

THE QUOTABLE MISES

MARK THORNTON, EDITOR

Ludwig
von Mises
Institute
AUBURN, ALABAMA

INTRODUCTION

Ludwig von Mises was one of the greatest thinkers of the 20th century. More than just an economist, Mises was an historian, philosopher, sociologist, social critic and so much more. His prolific output includes more than twenty books and hundreds of articles that explore virtually every subject of interest related to the economy and social thought.

It has become increasingly common for writers working for the financial publications, the popular press, mainstream academic journals, and most especially the Internet, to quote from the writing of Mises. He left us with a tremendous storehouse of knowledge to quote from. It remains fresh and insightful, so eminently applicable, and even entertaining. We hope this book will further encourage this trend.

The idea for this project was the brainchild of Martin Garfinkel, Esquire, of Carbondale, Colorado. He not only foresaw the need and usefulness of such a book, but collected an entire book's worth of quotations from *Human Action,* which was the starting point and forms the core of this book. It really has been a group project with several people making important contributions such as Thomas DiLorenzo, C.J. Maloney, and B.K. Marcus. Many scholars associated with the Mises Institute assisted, as well as the staff, especially Jeffrey Tucker, and many students. Of special note is Richard Perry who edited and collated the final list of quotes. The greatest thanks goes to Bettina Bien Greaves, whose enthusiastic support for this project provided inspiration. Her generous permission to use these quotes, as well as her suggestions along the way, are greatly appreciated.

This book is not intended as an introduction to Mises or as a summary of his work. It is only a collection of pithy quotations that illustrate the power of his thought.

One of the biggest hurdles was not finding good quotes, but limiting the number of quotes to a useful level. Mises's important books and monographs were mined for quotable material as we tried to provide a representative list of topics and subjects that Mises is most famous for: socialism, bureaucracy, interventionism, money, government, and war. We included many subject areas for which Mises is not often quoted, including arts, fate, health, instinct, martyrdom, religion, and youth.

We hope that you find your favorite Mises quote in this book, but we do not guarantee it. We could not even include all of our own favorites. Only the most minimal punctuation changes have been made and only for the literary demands of this venue. The page numbers are included so that the reader can examine the context and full import of all of these quotes.[1]

Enjoy.

Mark Thornton
Editor

Mark Thornton is a Senior Fellow at the Ludwig von Mises Institute and the book review editor for the *Quarterly Journal of Austrian Economics*. He is the author of *The Economics of Prohibition* and coauthor of *Tariffs, Blockades, and Inflation: The Economics of the Civil War* (with Robert B. Ekelund, Jr.).

[1]We have included page numbers for both the Scholar's Edition of *Human Action* (which is a reprint of the first edition) and the third edition. The quotes here have been taken from the more widely circulated third edition and in a few instances they are slightly different from the first edition. The page numbers appearing first in the text are from the first edition, followed by the page numbers from the third edition.

The Mises Institute is preparing a new translation of Mises's *Notes and Recollections*, and the quotes herein are from this new translation.

CONTENTS

ACTION

Human action is purposeful behavior.

Human Action, p. 11; p. 11

Human life is an unceasing sequence of single actions.

Human Action, p. 45; p. 45

Action is purposive conduct. It is not simply behavior, but behavior begot by judgments of value, aiming at a definite end and guided by ideas concerning the suitability or unsuitability of definite means. . . . It is conscious behavior. It is choosing. It is volition; it is a display of the will.

The Ultimate Foundation of Economic Science, p. 34

Man thinks not only for the sake of thinking, but also in order to act.

Epistemological Problems of Economics, p. 37

Economics, as a branch of the more general theory of human action, deals with all human action, i.e., with man's purposive aiming at the attainment of ends chosen, whatever these ends may be.

Human Action, p. 880; p. 884

Action is a display of potency and control that are limited. It is a manifestation of man who is restrained by the circumscribed powers of his mind, the physiological nature of his body, the vicissitudes of his environment, and the scarcity of external factors on which his welfare depends.

Human Action, p. 70; p. 70

Action is an attempt to substitute a more satisfactory state of affairs for a less satisfactory one. We call such a willfully induced alteration an exchange.

Human Action, p. 97; p. 97

Most actions do not aim at anybody's defeat or loss. They aim at an improvement in conditions.

Human Action, p. 116; p. 116

The vigorous man industriously striving for the improvement of his condition acts neither more nor less than the lethargic man who sluggishly takes things as they come. For to do nothing and to be idle are also action, they too determine the course of events.

Human Action, p. 13; p. 13

Man's striving after an improvement of the conditions of his existence impels him to action. Action requires planning and the decision which of various plans is the most advantageous.

The Ultimate Foundation of Economic Science, p. 90

In the land of the lotus-eaters there is no action. Action arises only from need, from dissatisfaction. It is purposeful striving towards something. Its ultimate end is always to get rid of a condition which is conceived to be deficient—to fulfill a need, to achieve satisfaction, to increase happiness.

Socialism, p. 97

All rational action is in the first place individual action. Only the individual thinks. Only the individual reasons. Only the individual acts.

Socialism, p. 97

ADVERTISING

It is a widespread fallacy that skillful advertising can talk the consumers into buying everything that the advertiser wants them to buy. The consumer is, according to this legend, simply defenseless against "high-pressure" advertising. If this were true, success or failure in business would depend on the mode of advertising only.

Human Action, p. 317; p. 321

The tricks and artifices of advertising are available to the seller of the better product no less than to the seller of the poorer product. But only the former enjoys the advantage derived from the better quality of his product.

Human Action, p. 318; p. 321

AMERICA

It is an enormous simplification to speak of the American mind. Every American has his own mind. It is absurd to ascribe any achievements and virtues or any misdeeds and vices of individual Americans to America as such. . . . What makes the American people different from any other people is the joint effect produced by the thoughts and actions of innumerable uncommon Americans.

Theory and History, pp. 191–92

Used to the conditions of a capitalistic environment, the average American takes it for granted that every year business makes something new and better accessible to him. Looking backward upon the years of his own life, he realizes that many implements that were totally unknown in the days of his youth and many others which at that time could be enjoyed only by a small minority are now standard equipment of almost every household. He is fully confident that this trend will prevail also in the future. He simply calls it the "American way of life" and does not give serious thought to the question of what made this continuous improvement in the supply of material goods possible.

Economic Freedom and Interventionism, p. 7

The most serious dangers for American freedom and the American way of life do not come from without.

Economic Freedom and Interventionism, p. 101

There is no use in deceiving ourselves. American public opinion rejects the market economy, the capitalistic free enterprise system that provided the nation with the highest standard of living ever attained. Full government control of all activities of the individual is virtually the goal of both national parties.

Economic Freedom and Interventionism, p. 157

ANIMALS

The nonhuman animals never proceed beyond instinctive urges and conditioned reflexes.

The Ultimate Foundation of Economic Science, p. 49

ANTI-SEMITISM

It was not the first time in French history that the nationalists put their anti-Semitism above their French patriotism. In the Dreyfus Affair they fought vigorously in order to let a treacherous officer quietly evade punishment while an innocent Jew languished in prison.

Omnipotent Government, p. 190

The Nazis have an ally in every town or village where there is a man eager to get rid of a Jewish competitor. The secret weapon of Hitler is the anti-Jewish inclinations of many millions of shopkeepers and grocers, of doctors and lawyers, professors and writers.

Omnipotent Government, p. 192

ANTITRUST LAWS

The consumers suffer when the laws of the country prevent the most efficient entrepreneurs from expanding the sphere of their activities. What made some enterprises develop into "big business" was precisely their success in filling best the demand of the masses.

Planned Chaos, p. 22

Those politicians, professors and union bosses who curse big business are fighting for a lower standard of living.

Theory and History, p. 147

ARCHITECTURE

In the last hundred years many churches and even cathedrals were built and many more government palaces, schools, and libraries. But they do not show any original conception; they reflect old styles or hybridize divers old styles. Only in apartment houses, office buildings and private homes have we seen something develop that may be qualified as an architectural style of our age. Although it would be mere pedantry not to appreciate the peculiar grandeur of such sights as the New York skyline, it can be admitted that modern architecture has not attained the distinction of that of past centuries.

The Anti-Capitalistic Mentality, p. 78

ARTS

The enjoyment of art and literature presupposes a certain disposition and susceptibility on the part of the public. Taste is inborn to only a few. Others must cultivate their aptitude for enjoyment.

Theory and History, p. 63

It is a purposeful distortion of facts to blame the age of liberalism for an alleged materialism. The nineteenth century was not only a century of unprecedented improvement in technical methods of production and in the material well-being of the masses. It did much more than extend the average length of human life. Its scientific and artistic accomplishments are imperishable. It was an age of immortal musicians, writers, poets, painters, and sculptors; it revolutionized philosophy, economics, mathematics, physics, chemistry, and biology. And, for the first time in history, it made the great works and the great thoughts accessible to the common man.

Human Action, p. 155; p. 155

Under capitalism, material success depends on the appreciation of a man's achievements on the part of the sovereign consumers. In this regard there is no difference between the services rendered by a manufacturer and those rendered by a producer, an actor or a playwright.

The Anti-Capitalistic Mentality, p. 31

There has never been an era in which the many were prepared to do justice to contemporary art. Reverence to the great authors and artists has always been limited to small groups.

The Anti-Capitalistic Mentality, p. 79

What characterizes capitalism is not the bad taste of the crowds, but the fact that these crowds, made prosperous by capitalism, became "consumers" of literature—of course, of trashy literature. The book market is flooded by a downpour of trivial fiction for the semibarbarians. But this does not prevent great authors from creating imperishable works.

The Anti-Capitalistic Mentality, p. 79

Only stilted pedants can conceive the idea that there are absolute norms to tell what is beautiful and what is not. They try to derive from the works of the past a code of rules with which, as they fancy, the writers and artists of the future should comply. But the genius does not cooperate with the pundit.

Theory and History, p. 63

Art is nothing more than a faltering and inadequate attempt to express what has been thus experienced and to give some form to its content. The work of art captures not the experience, but only what its creator has been able to express of the experience.

Epistemological Problems of Economics, p. 45

The most primitive work of art also can express the strongest experience, and it speaks to us, if only we let it.

Epistemological Problems of Economics, p. 46

A work of art is an attempt to experience the universe as a whole. One cannot analyze or dissect it into parts and comment on it without destroying its intrinsic character.

Epistemological Problems of Economics, p. 136

There can be no freedom in art and literature where the government determines who shall create them.

Omnipotent Government, p. 52

It is a hopeless task to interpret a symphony, a painting, or a novel. The interpreter at best tries to tell us something about his reaction to the work. He cannot tell us with certainty what the creator's meaning was or what other people may see in it. Even if the creator himself provides a commentary on his work, as in the case of program-music, this uncertainty remains. There are no words to describe the ineffable.

Theory and History, p. 276

Whom should the government entrust with the task of deciding whether a newcomer is really a great painter or not? It would have to rely on the judgment of the critics, and the professors of the history of art who are always looking back into the past yet who very rarely have shown the talent to discovery new genius.

Economic Policy, p. 31

AUSTRIAN ECONOMISTS

The main and only concern of the Austrian economists was to contribute to the advancement of economics. They never tried to win the support of anybody by other means than by the convincing power developed in their books and articles. They looked with indifference upon the fact that the universities of the German-speaking countries, even many of the Austrian universities, were hostile to economics as such and still more so to the new economic doctrines of subjectivism.

Austrian Economics: An Anthology, p. 72

Those whom the world called the "Austrian economists" were, in the Austrian universities, somewhat reluctantly tolerated outsiders.

Austrian Economics: An Anthology, p. 56

What distinguishes the Austrian School and will lend it everlasting fame is its doctrine of economic action, in contrast to one of economic equilibrium or nonaction.

Notes and Recollections, p. 36.

AUTOBIOGRAPHICAL

How one carries on in the face of unavoidable catastrophe is a matter of temperament. In high school, as was custom, I had chosen a verse by Virgil to be my motto: *Tu ne cede malis sed contra audentior ito.* "Do not give in to evil, but proceed ever more boldly against it." I recalled these words during the darkest hours of the war. Again and again I had met with situations from which rational deliberation found no means of escape; but then the unexpected intervened, and with it came salvation. I would not lose courage even now. I wanted to do everything an economist could do. I would not tire in saying what I knew to be true.

Notes and Recollections, p. 70

Otto Bauer was too bright not to realize that I was right, but he never forgave me for having turned him into a Millerand. The attacks of his fellow Bolshevists hit close to home, but he directed his animosity toward me instead of toward his opponents. A powerful loather, he opted for ignoble means to destroy me. He attempted to incite the nationalistic students and professors at the University of Vienna to turn against me. The assault miscarried.

Notes and Recollections, pp. 18–19

From time to time I entertained the hope that my writings would bear practical fruit and show the way for policy. I have always looked for evidence of a change in ideology. But I never actually deceived myself; my theories explain, but cannot slow the decline of a great civilization. I set out to be a reformer, but only became the historian of decline.

Notes and Recollections, p. 115

BANKING

There was no reason whatever to abandon the principle of free enterprise in the field of banking.

Human Action, p. 440; p. 443

It is extremely difficult for our contemporaries to conceive of the conditions of free banking because they take government interference with banking for granted and as necessary.

Human Action, p. 444; p. 447

What is needed to prevent any further credit expansion is to place the banking business under the general rules of commercial and civil laws compelling every individual and firm to fulfill all obligations in full compliance with the terms of the contract.

Human Action, p. 440; p. 443

Imprudent granting of credit is bound to prove just as ruinous to a bank as to any other merchant.

The Theory of Money and Credit, p. 295

BARBARISM

The social system of private property and limited government is the only system that tends to debarbarize all those who have the innate capacity to acquire personal culture.

Liberty and Property, p. 26

BEHAVIORISM

Behaviorism fails to explain why different people adjust themselves to the same conditions in different ways.

Theory and History, p. 245

Behaviorism proposes to study human behavior according to the methods developed by animal and infant psychology. It seeks to investigate reflexes and instincts, automatisms and unconscious reactions. But it has told us nothing about the reflexes that have built cathedrals, railroads, and fortresses, the instincts that have produced philosophies, poems, and legal systems, the automatisms that have resulted in the growth and decline of empires, the unconscious reactions that are splitting atoms.

Theory and History, pp. 245–46

BIG BUSINESS

The bigness and the economic "power" of the railroad companies did not impede the emergence of the motor car and the airplane.

Human Action, p. 276; p. 275

Big business always serves—directly or indirectly—the masses.

The Anti-Capitalistic Mentality, p. 2

Not offices and bureaucrats, but big business deserves credit for the fact that most of the families in the United States own a motorcar and a radio set.

Planned Chaos, p. 15

The big business enterprises are almost without exception corporations, precisely because they are too big for single individuals to own them entirely. The growth of business units has far outstripped the growth of individual fortunes.

Theory and History, p. 118

The characteristic mark of big business is mass production for the satisfaction of the needs of the masses. Under capitalism the workers themselves, directly or indirectly, are the main consumers of all those things that the factories are turning out.

The Anti-Capitalistic Mentality, p. 42

What makes a firm big is its success in best filling the demands of the buyers. If the bigger enterprise did not better serve the people than a smaller one, it would long since have been reduced to smallness.

Planning for Freedom, p. 134

Big business depends entirely on the patronage of those who buy its products: the biggest enterprises loses its power and its influence when it loses its customers.

Economic Policy, p. 4

BÖHM-BAWERK, EUGEN VON

There is no doubt that Böhm-Bawerk's book is the most eminent contribution to modern economic theory. For every economist it is a must to study it most carefully and to scrutinize its content with the utmost care. A man not perfectly familiar with all the ideas advanced in these three volumes has no claim whatever to the appellation of an economist.

Economic Freedom and Interventionism, p. 133

A book of the size and profundity of *Capital and Interest* is not easy reading. But the effort expended pays very well. It will stimulate the reader to look upon political problems, not from the point of view of the superficial slogans resorted to in electoral campaigns, but with full awareness of their meaning and their consequences for the survival of our civilization.

Economic Freedom and Interventionism, p. 135

BORDERS

[In a liberal world] it makes no difference where the frontiers of a country are drawn. Nobody has a special material interest in enlarging the territory of the state in which he lives; nobody suffers loss if part of this area is separated from the state. It is also immaterial whether all parts of the state's territory are in direct geographical connection, or whether they are separated by a piece of land belonging to another state. It is of no economic importance whether the country has a frontage on the ocean or not. In such a world the people of every village or district could decide by plebiscite to which state they want to belong.

Omnipotent Government, p. 92

BOURGEOISIE

The much abused "shopkeepers" have abolished slavery and serfdom, made woman the companion of man with equal rights, proclaimed equality before the law and freedom of thought and opinion, declared war on war, abolished torture, and mitigated the cruelty of punishment. What cultural force can boast of similar achievements? Bourgeois civilization has created and spread a well-being, compared with which all the court life of the past seems meagre.

Socialism, p. 398

Through all the changes in the prevailing system of social stratification, moral philosophers continued to hold fast to the fundamental idea of Cicero's doctrine that making money is degrading.

Epistemological Problems of Economics, p. 194

BUREAUCRACY

The worst law is better than bureaucratic tyranny.

Bureaucracy, p. 76

In all countries with a settled bureaucracy people used to say: The cabinets come and go, but the bureaus remain.

Bureaucracy, p. 55

Bureaucratic management is management of affairs which cannot be checked by economic calculation.

Bureaucracy, p. 48

Nobody can be at the same time a correct bureaucrat and an innovator.

Bureaucracy, p. 67

The ultimate basis of an all around bureaucratic system is violence.

Bureaucracy, p. 104

Seen from the point of view of the particular group interests of the bureaucrats, every measure that makes the government's payroll swell is progress.

Planning for Freedom, p. 48

If you have to convince a group of people who are not directly dependent on a solution of a problem, you will never succeed.

Economic Policy, pp. 30–31

A government enterprise can never be "commercialized" no matter how many external features of private enterprise are superimposed on it.

A Critique of Interventionism, p. 159

They are no longer eager to deal with each case to the best of their abilities; they are no longer anxious to find the most appropriate solution for every problem. Their main concern is to comply with the rules and regulations, no matter whether they are reasonable or contrary to what was intended. The first virtue of an administrator is to abide by the codes and decrees.

Bureaucracy, p. 41

Bureaucratic conduct of affairs is conduct bound to comply with detailed rules and regulations fixed by the authority of a superior body. It is the only alternative to profit management. . . . Whenever the operation of a system is not directed by the profit motive, it must be directed by bureaucratic rules.

Human Action, p. 307; p. 310

The bureaucrat is not free to aim at improvement. He is bound to obey rules and regulations established by a superior body. He has no right to embark upon innovations if his superiors do not approve of them. His duty and his virtue is to be obedient.

Bureaucracy, p. 66

A bureaucrat differs from a nonbureaucrat precisely because he is working in a field in which it is impossible to appraise the result of a man's effort in terms of money.

Bureaucracy, p. 53

Of course, the bulk of the bureaucrats were rather mediocre men.

Bureaucracy, p. 56

Progress of any kind is always at variance with the old and established ideas and therefore with the codes inspired by them. Every step of progress is a change involving heavy risks.

Bureaucracy, p. 67

Only to bureaucrats can the idea occur that establishing new offices, promulgating new decrees, and increasing the number of government employees alone can be described as positive and beneficial measures.

Omnipotent Government, p. x

The public firm can nowhere maintain itself in free competition with the private firm; it is possible today only where it has a monopoly that excludes competition. Even that alone is evidence of its lesser economic productivity.

Nation, State, and Economy, p. 186

The trend toward bureaucratic rigidity is not inherent in the evolution of business. It is an outcome of government meddling with business.

Bureaucracy, p. 12

No private enterprise will ever fall prey to bureaucratic methods of management if it is operated with the sole aim of making profit.

Bureaucracy, p. 64

BUSINESS CYCLES

If one wants to avoid the recurrence of economic crises, one must avoid the expansion of credit that creates the boom and inevitably leads into the slump.

The Theory of Money and Credit, p. 482

The ultimate cause, therefore, of the phenomenon of wave after wave of economic ups and downs is ideological in character. The cycles will not disappear so long as people believe that the rate of interest may be reduced, not through the accumulation of capital, but by banking policy.

On the Manipulation of Money and Credit, p. 139

Credit expansion can bring about a temporary boom. But such a fictitious prosperity must end in a general depression of trade, a slump.

Planned Chaos, p. 21

The cyclical fluctuations of business are not an occurrence originating in the sphere of the unhampered market, but a product of government interference with business conditions designed to lower the rate of interest below the height at which the free market would have fixed it.

Human Action, p. 562; p. 565

True, governments can reduce the rate of interest in the short run. They can issue additional paper money. They can open the way to credit expansion by the banks. They can thus create an artificial boom and the appearance of prosperity. But such a boom is bound to collapse soon or late and to bring about a depression.

Omnipotent Government, p. 251

The wavelike movement effecting the economic system, the recurrence of periods of boom which are followed by periods of depression is the unavoidable outcome of the attempts, repeated again and again, to lower the gross market rate of interest by means of credit expansion.

Human Action, p. 570; p. 572

The boom produces impoverishment. But still more disastrous are its moral ravages. It makes people despondent and dispirited. The more optimistic they were under the illusory prosperity of the boom, the greater is their despair and their feeling of frustration. The individual is always ready to ascribe his good luck to his own efficiency and to take it as a well-deserved reward for his talent, application and probity. But reverses of fortune he always charges to other people, and most of all to the absurdity of social and political institutions. He does not blame the authorities for having fostered the boom. He reviles them for the inevitable collapse.

Human Action, p. 574; p. 576

BUSINESSMEN

Of course, as a rule capitalists and entrepreneurs are not saints excelling in the virtue of self-denial. But neither are their critics saintly.

Planning for Freedom, p. 146

CALCULATION

Monetary calculation and cost accounting constitute the most important intellectual tool of the capitalist entrepreneur, and it was no one less than Goethe who pronounced the system of double-entry bookkeeping "one of the finest inventions of the human mind." Goethe could say this because he was free from the resentment that the petty literati always foster against the businessman.

Liberalism, p. 97

Economic calculation makes it possible for business to adjust production to the demands of the consumers.

Bureaucracy, p. 27

Accountancy is not perfect. The precision of its statements is only illusory. The valuations of goods and rights with which it deals are always based on estimates depending on more or less uncertain and unknown factors.

The Theory of Money and Credit, p. 234

The elaborate methods of modern bookkeeping, accountancy, and business statistics provide the enterpriser with a faithful image of all his operations. He is in a position to learn how successful or unsuccessful every one of his transactions was.

Bureaucracy, p. 32

CAPITAL

Now nobody ever contended that one could produce without working. But neither is it possible to produce without capital goods, the previously produced factors of further production.

Planning for Freedom, p. 111

What the workers must learn is that the only reason why wage rates are higher in the United States is that the per head quota of capital invested is higher.

Planning for Freedom, p. 92

There are no means by which the general standard of living can be raised other than by accelerating the increase of capital as compared with population.

Planning for Freedom, pp. 5–6

In a given economic situation, the opportunities for production, which may actually be carried out, are limited by the supply of capital goods available.

On the Manipulation of Money and Credit, p. 125

It is nonsensical to impute the whole product to the purveyors of labor and to pass over in silence the contribution of the purveyors of capital and of entrepreneurial ideas. What brings forth usable goods is not physical effort as such, but physical effort aptly directed by the human mind toward a definite goal.

Human Action, No Entry; p. 301

All capital goods sooner or later enter into final products and cease to exist through use, consumption, wear and tear.

Human Action, p. 514; p. 517

Profit-seeking business is compelled to employ the most efficient methods of production. What checks a businessman's endeavors to improve the equipment of his firm is only lack of capital.

Human Action, p. 769; p. 775

All the effusions of the contemporary welfare school are, like those of the socialist authors, based on the implicit assumption that there is an abundant supply of capital goods. Then, of course, it seems easy to find a remedy for all ills, to give to everybody "according to his needs" and to make everyone perfectly happy.

Human Action, p. 844; p. 848

When pushed hard by economists, some welfare propagandists and socialists admit that impairment of the average standard of living can only be avoided by the maintenance of capital already accumulated and that economic improvement depends on accumulation of additional capital.

Human Action, p. 844; p. 848

History does not provide any example of capital accumulation brought about by a government. As far as governments invested in the construction of roads, railroads, and other useful public works, the capital needed was provided by the savings of individual citizens and borrowed by the government.

Human Action, p. 847; p. 851

Capital does not reproduce itself.

Socialism, p. 177

CAPITALISM

The characteristic mark of economic history under capitalism is unceasing economic progress, a steady increase in the quantity of capital goods available, and a continuous trend toward an improvement in the general standard of living.

Human Action, p. 562; p. 565

The characteristic feature of capitalism that distinguishes it from pre-capitalist methods of production was its new principle of marketing. Capitalism is not simply mass production, but mass production to satisfy the needs of the masses.

Liberty and Property, p. 9

Capitalism or market economy is that system of social cooperation and division of labor that is based on private ownership of the means of production.

Bureaucracy, p. 20

Capitalism is essentially a system of mass production for the satisfaction of the needs of the masses. It pours a horn of plenty upon the common man. It has raised the average standard of living to a height never dreamed of in earlier ages. It has made accessible to millions of people enjoyments which a few generations ago were only within the reach of a small élite.

The Anti-Capitalistic Mentality, p. 49

The early industrialists were for the most part men who had their origin in the same social strata from which their workers came. They lived very modestly, spent only a fraction of their earnings for their households and put the rest back into the business.

Human Action, p. 617; p. 622

Many pioneers of these industrial changes, it is true, became rich. But they acquired their wealth by supplying the public with motor cars, airplanes, radio sets, refrigerators, moving and talking pictures, and variety of less spectacular but no less useful innovations. These new products were certainly not an achievement of offices and bureaucrats.

Omnipotent Government, pp. ix–x

The development of capitalism consists in everyone having the right to serve the consumer better and/or more cheaply.

Economic Policy, p. 5

There is no western, capitalistic country in which the conditions of the masses have not improved in an unprecedented way.

Economic Policy, p. 13

In spite of the anticapitalistic policies of all governments and of almost all political parties, the capitalist mode of production is still fulfilling its social function in supplying the consumers with more, better and cheaper goods.

Planned Chaos, p. 15

It is inherent in the nature of the capitalistic economy that, in the final analysis, the employment of the factors of production is aimed only toward serving the wishes of consumers.

On the Manipulation of Money and Credit, p. 176

The capitalistic social order, therefore, is an economic democracy in the strictest sense of the word. In the last analysis, all decisions are dependent on the will of the people as consumers. Thus, whenever there is a conflict between the consumers' views and those of the business managers, market pressures assure that the views of the consumers win out eventually.

On the Manipulation of Money and Credit, p. 178

Grumblers may blame Western civilization for its materialism and may assert that it gratified nobody but a small class of rugged exploiters. But their laments cannot wipe out the facts. Millions of mothers have been made happier by the drop in infant mortality. Famines have disappeared and epidemics have been curbed. The average man lives in more satisfactory conditions than his ancestors or his fellows in noncapitalistic countries. And one must not dismiss as merely materialistic a civilization which makes it possible for practically everybody to enjoy a Beethoven symphony performed by an orchestra conducted by an eminent master.

Theory and History, p. 334

The capitalist system of production is an economic democracy in which every penny gives a right to vote. The consumers are the sovereign people. The capitalists, the entrepreneurs, and the farmers are the people's mandatories. If they do not obey, if they fail to produce, at the lowest possible cost, what the consumers are asking for, they lose their office. Their task is service to the consumer. Profit and loss are the instruments by means of which the consumers keep a tight rein on all business activities.

Bureaucracy, pp. 21–22

A short time ago the demagogues blamed capitalism for the poverty of the masses. Today they rather blame capitalism for the "affluence" that it bestows upon the common man.

Human Action, No Entry; p. 859

Capitalism gave the world what it needed, a higher standard of living for a steadily increasing number of people.

Human Action, pp. 860–61; p. 864

The word "Capitalism" expresses, for our age, the sum of all evil. Even the opponents of Socialism are dominated by socialist ideas.

Socialism, p. 15

In the capitalist society there is a place and bread for all. Its ability to expand provides sustenance for every worker. Permanent unemployment is not a feature of free capitalism.

Socialism, p. 286

We do not assert that the capitalist mode of economic calculation guarantees the absolutely best solution of the allocation of factors of production. Such absolutely perfect solutions of any problem are out of reach of mortal men. What the operation of a market not sabotaged by the interference of compulsion and coercion can bring about is merely the best solution accessible to the human mind under the given state of technological knowledge and the intellectual abilities of the age's shrewdest men.

Human Action, p. 701; p. 705

The market economy needs no apologists and propagandists. It can apply to itself the words of Sir Christopher Wren's epitaph in St. Paul's: *Si monumentum requiris, circumspice.* [If you seek his monument, look around.]

Human Action, p. 850; p. 854

All the talk about the so-called unspeakable horror of early capitalism can be refuted by a single statistic: precisely in these years in which British capitalism developed, precisely in the age called the Industrial Revolution in England, in the years from 1760 to 1830, precisely in those years the population of England doubled.

Economic Policy, p. 7

The market economy—capitalism—is a social system of consumers' supremacy.

Money, Method, and the Market Process, p. 233

Capitalism needs neither propaganda nor apostles. Its achievements speak for themselves. Capitalism delivers the goods.

Money, Method, and the Market Process, p. 242

CAPITALISM VS. SOCIALISM

The issue is always the same: the government or the market. There is no third solution.

Planned Chaos, p. 28

Capitalism and socialism are two distinct patterns of social organization. Private control of the means of production and public control are contradictory notions and not merely contrary notions. There is no such thing as a mixed economy, a system that would stand midway between capitalism and socialism.

The Anti-Capitalistic Mentality, pp. 64–65

Capitalism means free enterprise, sovereignty of the consumers in economic matters, and sovereignty of the voters in political matters. Socialism means full government control of every sphere of the individual's life and the unrestricted supremacy of the government in its capacity as central board of production management. There is no compromise possible between these two systems. Contrary to a popular fallacy there is no middle way, no third system possible as a pattern of a permanent social order. The citizens must choose between capitalism and socialism.

Bureaucracy, p. 10

If one rejects laissez faire on account of man's fallibility and moral weakness, one must for the same reason also reject every kind of government action.

Planning for Freedom, p. 44

Tyranny is the political corollary of socialism, as representative government is the political corollary of the market economy.

Planning for Freedom, p. 218

A society that chooses between capitalism and socialism does not choose between two social systems; it chooses between social cooperation and the disintegration of society. Socialism: is not an alternative to capitalism; it is an alternative to any system under which men can live as *human* beings.

Human Action, p. 676; p. 680

The desire for an increase of wealth can be satisfied through exchange, which is the only method possible in a capitalist economy, or by violence and petition as in a militarist society, where the strong acquire by force, the weak by petitioning.

Socialism, p. 335

For it is an essential difference between capitalist and social-ist production that under capitalism men provide for them-selves, while under Socialism they are provided for.

Socialism, p. 405

[Classical] Liberalism and capitalism address themselves to the cool, well-balanced mind. They proceed by strict logic, eliminating any appeal to the emotions. Socialism, on the con-trary, works on the emotions, tries to violate logical considera-tions by rousing a sense of personal interest and to stifle the voice of reason by awakening primitive instincts.

Socialism, p. 460

The salesman thanks the customer for patronizing his shop and asks him to come again. But the socialists say: Be grateful to Hitler, render thanks to Stalin; be nice and submissive, then the great man will be kind to you later too.

Omnipotent Government, p. 53

There is simply no other choice than this: either to abstain from interference in the free play of the market, or to delegate the entire management of production and distribution to the govern-ment. Either capitalism or socialism: there exists no middle way.

Liberalism, p. 79

CAUSE AND EFFECT

Cognizance of the relation between a cause and its effect is the first step toward man's orientation in the world and is the intellectual condition of any successful activity.

The Ultimate Foundation of Economic Science, p. 20

CENSORSHIP

Everybody is free to abstain from reading books, magazines, and newspapers he dislikes and to recommend to other people to shun these books, magazines, and newspapers. But it is quite another thing when some people threaten other people with serious reprisals in case they should not stop patronizing certain publications and their publishers.

The Anti-Capitalistic Mentality, p. 56

CHANGE

The great mass of people are incapable of realizing that in economic life nothing is permanent except change. They regard the existing state of affairs as eternal; as it has been so shall it always be.

Socialism, p. 188

In life everything is continually in flux.

Epistemological Problems of Economics, p. 108

There is never a standstill in the economy, but perpetual changes, movement, innovation, the continual emergence of the unprecedented.

Liberalism, p. 80

CHARITY

We may fully endorse the religious and ethical precepts that declare it to be man's duty to assist his unlucky brethren whom nature has doomed. But the recognition of this duty does not answer the question concerning what methods should be resorted to for its performance.

Human Action, p. 835; p. 839

No civilized community has callously allowed the incapacitated to perish. But the substitution of a legally enforceable claim to support or sustenance for charitable relief does not seem to agree with human nature as it is. Not metaphysical prepossessions, but considerations of practical expediency make it inadvisable to promulgate an actionable right to sustenance. It is, moreover, an illusion to believe that the enactment of such laws could free the indigent from the degrading features inherent in receiving alms. The more openhanded these laws are, the more punctilious must their application become. The discretion of bureaucrats is substituted for the discretion of people whom an inner voice drives to acts of charity.

Human Action, pp. 835–36; pp. 839–40

CHAUVINISM

Every sort of chauvinism is mistaken.

Liberalism, p. 144

As long as nations cling to protective tariffs, migration barriers, compulsory education, interventionism and etatism, new conflicts capable of breaking out at any time into open warfare will continually arise to plague mankind.

Liberalism, pp. 150–51

Conceit and overvaluation of one's own nation are quite common. But it would be wrong to assume that hatred and contempt of foreigners are natural and innate qualities. Even soldiers fighting to kill their enemies do not hate the individual foe, if they happen to meet him apart from the battle.

Omnipotent Government, p. 124

Chauvinism has not begotten nationalism. Its chief function in the scheme of nationalist policies is to adorn the shows and festivals of nationalism. People overflow with joy and pride when the official speakers hail them as the elite of mankind and praise the immortal deeds of their ancestors and the invincibility of their armed forces. But when the words fade away and the celebration reaches its end, people return home and go to bed. They do not mount the battlehorse.

Omnipotent Government, p. 125

CHOICE

Man is not, like the animals, an obsequious puppet of instincts and sensual impulses. Man has the power to suppress instinctive desires, he has a will of his own, he chooses between incompatible ends.

The Ultimate Foundation of Economic Science, p. 57

While all other animals are unconditionally driven by the impulse to preserve their own lives and by the impulse of proliferation, man has the power to master even these impulses.

He can control both his sexual desires and his will to live. He can give up his life when the conditions under which alone he could preserve it seem intolerable. Man is capable of dying for a cause or of committing suicide. To live is for man the outcome of a choice, of a judgment of value.

Human Action, p. 19; pp. 19–20

Choosing ultimate ends is a personal, subjective, individual affair. Choosing means is a matter of reason, choosing ultimate ends a matter of the soul and the will.

Theory and History, p. 15

CHRISTIANITY

Since the third century Christianity has always served simultaneously those who supported the social order and those who wished to overthrow it. . . . It is the same today: Christianity fights both for and against Socialism.

Socialism, p. 378

It was not the Syllabus of Pope Pius IX that paved the way for the return of intolerance and the persecution of dissenters. It was the writings of the socialists.

Theory and History, p. 68

Christian Socialism is none the less Socialism.

Socialism, p. 382

Christianity has acquiesced in slavery and polygamy, has practically canonized war, has, in the name of the Lord, burnt heretics and devastated countries.

Socialism, pp. 397–98

Virtually all the Christian churches and sects have espoused the principles of socialism and interventionism. In almost every country the clergy favor nationalism. In spite of the fact that Catholicism is world embracing, even the Roman Church offers no exception. The nationalism of the Irish, the Poles, and the Slovaks is to a great extent an achievement of the clergy. French nationalism found most effective support in the Church.

Omnipotent Government, p. 120

Protestantism is no more a safeguard of freedom than Catholicism. The ideal of liberalism is the complete separation of church and state, and tolerance—without any regard to differences among the churches.

Omnipotent Government, p. 30

CHURCHILL, WINSTON

Great Britain was not brought to socialism by the Labour government which was established in 1945. Great Britain became socialist *during* the war, through the government of which Sir Winston Churchill was the prime minister. The Labour government simply retained the system of socialism which the government of Sir Winston Churchill had already introduced. And this in spite of great resistance by the people.

Economic Policy, p. 49

CIVIL SERVICE

It kills ambition, destroys initiative and the incentive to do more than the minimum required. It makes the bureaucrat look at instructions, not at material and real success.

Bureaucracy, p. 56

Most people joined the staff of the government offices because the salary and the pension offered were higher than what they could expect to earn in other occupations. They did not renounce anything in serving the government. Civil service was for them the most profitable job they could find.

Bureaucracy, p. 79

Representative democracy cannot subsist if a great part of the voters are on the government pay roll. If the members of parliament no longer consider themselves mandatories of the taxpayers but deputies of those receiving salaries, wages, subsidies, doles, and other benefits from the treasury, democracy is done for.

Bureaucracy, p. 81

Experience shows that nothing is operated with less economy and with more waste of labor and material of every kind than public services and undertakings. Private enterprise on the other hand naturally induces the owner to work with the greatest economy in his own interest.

Socialism, p. 160

The interventionist policy provides thousands and thousands of people with safe, placid, and not too strenuous jobs at the expense of the rest of society.

Socialism, p. 457

CIVILIZATION

What distinguishes civilized man from a barbarian must be acquired by every individual anew.

Theory and History, p. 293

What distinguishes man from animals is the insight into the advantages that can be derived from cooperation under the division of labor. Man curbs his innate instinct of aggression in order to cooperate with other human beings. The more he wants to improve his material well-being, the more he must expand the system of the division of labor.

Human Action, p. 827; p. 831

Modern civilization is a product of the philosophy of laissez faire. It cannot be preserved under the ideology of government omnipotence.

Human Action, p. 828; p. 832

Civilization is a product of leisure and the peace of mind that only the division of labour can make possible.

Socialism, p. 271

For society is nothing but collaboration.

Socialism, p. 281

Civilization is a work of peaceful co-operation.

Socialism, p. 291

Man is born an asocial and antisocial being. The newborn child is a savage. Egoism is his nature. Only the experience of life and the teachings of his parents, his brothers, sisters, play-mates, and later of other people force him to acknowledge the advantages of social cooperation and accordingly to change his behavior. The savage thus turns toward civilization and citizen-ship.

Omnipotent Government, p. 241

The foundation of any and every civilization, including our own, is private ownership of the means of production. Whoever wishes to criticize modern civilization, therefore, begins with private property.

Liberalism, p. 63

Modern civilization will not perish unless it does so by its own act of self-destruction. No external enemy can destroy it the way the Spaniards once destroyed the civilization of the Aztecs, for no one on earth can match his strength against the standard-bearers of modern civilization. Only inner enemies can threaten it. It can come to an end only if the ideas of liberalism are supplanted by an antiliberal ideology hostile to social cooperation.

Liberalism, pp. 188–89

CLASSES

No proletarian contributed anything to the construction of antiliberal teachings. At the root of the genealogical tree of modern socialism we meet the name of the depraved scion of one of the most eminent aristocratic families of royal France.

Omnipotent Government, p. 118

It is not true that the dangers to the maintenance of peace, democracy, freedom, and capitalism are a result of a "revolt of the masses." They are an achievement of scholars and intellectuals, of sons of the well-to-do, of writers and artists pampered by the best society. In every country of the world dynasties and aristocrats have worked with the socialists and interventionists against freedom.

Omnipotent Government, p. 119

The elite should be supreme by virtue of persuasion, not by the assistance of firing squads.

Omnipotent Government, p. 120

CLASS MOBILITY

In the feudal society, men became rich by war and conquest and through the largess of the sovereign ruler. Men became poor if they were defeated in battle or if they fell from the monarch's good graces. In the capitalistic society, men become rich—directly as the producer of consumers' goods, or indirectly as the producer of raw materials and semi-produced factors of production—by serving consumers in large numbers. This means that men who became rich in the capitalistic society are serving the people.

On the Manipulation of Money and Credit, pp. 177–78

In the unhampered market economy there are no privileges, no protection of vested interests, no barriers preventing anybody from striving after any prize.

Theory and History, p. 114

Entrance into the ranks of the entrepreneurs in a market society, not sabotaged by the interference of government or other agencies resorting to violence, is open to everybody.

Planning for Freedom, p. 117

Under capitalism everybody is the architect of his own fortune.

Bureaucracy, p. 100

CLASSICAL LIBERALISM

Economic knowledge necessarily leads to liberalism.

A Critique of Interventionism, p. 86

Several generations of economic policy which was nearly liberal have enormously increased the wealth of the world.

Socialism, p. 13

For Liberalism has never pretended to be more than a philosophy of earthly life. What it teaches is concerned only with earthly action and desistance from action. It has never claimed to exhaust the Last or Greatest Secret of Man.

Socialism, p. 37

Liberalism champions private property in the means of production because it expects a higher standard of living from such an economic organization, not because it wishes to help the owners.

Socialism, p. 46

That Liberalism aims at the protection of property and that it rejects war are two expressions of one and the same principle.

Socialism, p. 59

The only task of the strictly Liberal state is to secure life and property against attacks both from external and internal foes.

Socialism, p. 133

Freedom, democracy, peace, and private property are deemed good because they are the best means for promoting human happiness and welfare. Liberalism wants to secure to man a life free from fear and want. That is all.

Omnipotent Government, p. 51

The main excellence of the liberal scheme of social, economic, and political organization is precisely this—that it makes the peaceful cooperation of nations possible.

Omnipotent Government, p. 91

Imagine a world order in which liberalism is supreme . . . there is private property in the means of production. The working of the market is not hampered by government interference. There are no trade barriers; men can live and work where they want. Frontiers are drawn on the maps but they do not hinder the migrations of men and shipping of commodities. Natives do not enjoy rights that are denied to aliens. . . . The courts are independent and effectively protect everybody against the encroachments of officialdom. Everyone is permitted to say, to write, and to print what he likes. Education is not subject to government interference. . . . The men in office are regarded as mortal men, not as superhuman beings or as paternal authorities who have the right and duty to hold the people in tutelage. Governments do not have the power to dictate to the citizens.

Omnipotent Government, pp. 91–92

To the man who adopts the scientific method in reflecting upon the problems of human action, liberalism must appear as the only policy that can lead to lasting well-being for himself, his friends, and his loved ones, and, indeed, for all others as well. Only one who does not want to achieve such ends as life, health, and prosperity for himself, his friends, and those he loves, only one who prefers sickness, misery, and suffering may reject the reasoning of liberalism.

Epistemological Problems of Economics, p. 39

COERCION

All attempts to coerce the living will of human beings into the service of something they do not want must fail.

Socialism, p. 263

Economic affairs cannot be kept going by magistrates and policemen.

The Theory of Money and Credit, p. 282

COLLECTIVISM

It is not mankind, the state, or the corporative unit that acts, but individual men and groups of men, and *their* valuations and *their* action are decisive, not those of abstract collectivities.

Epistemological Problems of Economics, p. 153

The main characteristic of collectivism is that it does not take notice of the individual's will and moral self-determination.

The Ultimate Foundation of Economic Science, p. 106

Collectivism is a doctrine of war, intolerance, and persecution. If any of the collectivist creeds should succeed in its endeavors, all people but the great dictator would be deprived of their essential human quality. They would become mere soulless pawns in the hands of a monster.

Theory and History, p. 61

Society does not exist apart from the thoughts and actions of people. It does not have "interests" and does not aim at anything. The same is valid for all other collectives.

The Ultimate Foundation of Economic Science, p. 79

The collectivists idolize only the one true church, only the "great" nation . . . only the true state; everything else they condemn. For that reason all collectivists doctrines are harbingers of irreconcilable hatred and war to the death.

Epistemological Problems of Economics, p. 42

When the collectivist extols the state, what he means is not every state but only that regime of which he approves, no matter whether this legitimate state exists already or has to be created.

Theory and History, p. 254

COLONIALISM

No chapter of history is steeped further in blood than the history of colonialism. Blood was shed uselessly and senselessly. Flourishing lands were laid waste; whole peoples destroyed and exterminated. All this can in no way be extenuated or justified.

Liberalism, p. 125

It may be safely taken for granted that up to now the natives have learned only evil ways from the Europeans, and not good ones. This is not the fault of the natives, but rather of their European conquerors, who have taught them nothing but evil. They have brought arms and engines of destruction of all kinds to the colonies; they have sent out their worst and most brutal individuals as officials and officers; at the point of the sword they have set up a colonial rule that in its sanguinary cruelty rivals the despotic system of the Bolsheviks.

Liberalism, p. 126

The marvelous achievements of the British administration in India were overshadowed by the vain arrogance and stupid race pride of the white man. Asia is in open revolt against the gentlemen for whom socially there was but little difference between a dog and a native. . . . But it is at the same time the manifest failure of the greatest experiment in benevolent absolutism ever put to work.

Omnipotent Government, p. 98

The initiative for the great colonial projects came not from finance and business but from the governments.

Omnipotent Government, p. 99

COMMUNISM

In regard to economic policy, socialism and communism are identical.

Nation, State, and Economy, p. 178 n

A sound monetary policy is one of the foremost means to thwart the insidious schemes of communism.

Economic Freedom and Interventionism, p. 106

COMPETITION

Competition takes place among producers and sellers not only within each individual branch of production, but also between all related goods, and in the final analysis, between all economic goods.

A Critique of Interventionism, p. 48

Competitors aim at excellence and preeminence in accomplishments within a system of mutual cooperation. The function of competition is to assign to every member of the social system that position in which he can best serve the whole of society and all its members.

Human Action, p. 117; p. 117

The sharper the competition, the better it serves its social function to improve economic production.

A Critique of Interventionism, p. 84

It is merely a metaphor to call competition competitive war, or simply, war. The function of battle is destruction; of competition, construction.

Socialism, p. 285

CONFLICT

Class consciousness, created by the ideology of the class conflict, is the essence of the struggle, and not vice versa. The idea created the class, not the class the idea.

Socialism, p. 306

There are no irreconcilable conflicts between selfishness and altruism, between economics and ethics, between the concerns of the individual and those of society.

Theory and History, pp. 54–55

CONSCRIPTION

In relation to the immense sacrifices that the state demands of the individual through the blood tax, it seems rather incidental whether it compensates the soldier more or less abundantly for the loss of time that he suffers from his military-service obligation.

Nation, State, and Economy, p. 165

The first step which led from the soldiers' war back to total war was the introduction of compulsory military service. It gradually did away with the difference between soldiers and citizens.

Interventionism, pp. 69–70

Compulsory military service thus leads to compulsory labor service of all citizens who are able to work, male and female. . . . Mobilization has become total; the nation and the state have been transformed into an army; war socialism has replaced the market economy.

Interventionism, pp. 69–70

CONSERVATISM

Great Britain would not have gone socialist if the Conservatives, not to speak of the "Liberals," had not virtually endorsed socialist ideas.

Theory and History, p. 319n

The essence of an individual's freedom is the opportunity to deviate from traditional ways of thinking and of doing things.

Theory and History, p. 378

Every conservative policy, however, is fated from the start to fail; after all, its essence is to stop something unstoppable, to resist a development that cannot be impeded.

Nation, State, and Economy, p. 119

Every reactionary lacks intellectual independence.

Nation, State, and Economy, p. 119

A return to the Middle Ages is out of the question if one is not prepared to reduce the population to a tenth or a twentieth part of its present number and, even further, to oblige every individual to be satisfied with a modicum so small as to be beyond the imagination of modern man.

Liberalism, p. 86

What transformed the stagnant conditions of the good old days into the activism of capitalism was not changes in the natural sciences and in technology, but the adoption of the free enterprise principle.

The Ultimate Foundation of Economic Science, p. 122

CONSTITUTIONAL GOVERNMENT

There is really no essential difference between the unlimited power of the democratic state and the unlimited power of the autocrat. The idea that carries away our demagogues and their supporters, the idea that the state can do whatever it wishes, and that nothing should resist the will of the sovereign people, has done more evil perhaps than the caesar-mania of degenerate princelings.

Socialism, pp. 64–65

CONSUMER

The real bosses, in the capitalist system of market economy, are the consumers. They, by their buying and by their abstention from buying, decide who should own the capital and run the plants. They determine what should be produced and in what quantity and quality. Their attitudes result either in profit or in loss for the enterpriser. They make poor men rich and rich men poor. They are no easy bosses.

Bureaucracy, pp. 20–21

Those underlings who in all the preceding ages of history had formed the herds of slaves and serfs, of paupers and beggars, became the buying public, for whose favor the businessmen canvass. They are the customers who are "always right," the patrons who have the power to make poor suppliers rich and rich suppliers poor.

The Anti-Capitalistic Mentality, p. 2

The consumers are merciless. They never buy in order to benefit a less efficient producer and to protect him against the consequences of his failure to manage better. They want to be served as well as possible. And the working of the capitalist system forces the entrepreneur to obey the orders issued by the consumers.

Bureaucracy, p. 37

CONSUMER SOVEREIGNTY

Go into the home of the average American family and you will see for whom the wheels of the machines are turning.

Liberty and Property, p. 22

What vitiates entirely the socialists' economic critique of capitalism is their failure to grasp the sovereignty of the consumers in the market economy.

Liberty and Property, p. 13

CORRUPTION

The evil that a man inflicts on his fellow man injures both—not only the one to whom it is done, but also the one who does it. Nothing corrupts a man so much as being an arm of the law and making men suffer.

Liberalism, p. 58

There is no such thing as a just and fair method of exercising the tremendous power that interventionism puts into the hands of the legislature and the executive.

Human Action, No Entry; p. 734

In many fields of the administration of interventionist measures, favoritism simply cannot be avoided.

Human Action, No Entry; p. 735

Corruption is a regular effect of interventionism.

Human Action, No Entry; p. 736

The corruption of the regulatory bodies does not shake his blind confidence in the infallibility and perfection of the state; it merely fills him with moral aversion to entrepreneurs and capitalists.

A Critique of Interventionism, p. 30

Corruption is an evil inherent in every government not controlled by a watchful public opinion.

Omnipotent Government, p. 206

CREATIVITY

The essence of an individual's freedom is the opportunity to deviate from traditional ways of thinking and of doing things.

Theory and History, p. 378

Only the human mind that directs action and production is creative.

Human Action, p.141; p. 141

CREDIT

Credit transactions are in fact nothing but the exchange of present goods against future goods.

The Theory of Money and Credit, p. 47

Credit expansion is not a nostrum to make people happy. The boom it engenders must inevitably lead to a debacle and unhappiness.

Planning for Freedom, p. 189

No one should expect that any logical argument or any experience could ever shake the almost religious fervor of those who believe in salvation through spending and credit expansion.

Planning for Freedom, p. 63

The essence of a credit-expansion boom is not overinvestment, but investment in wrong lines, i.e., malinvestment.

Human Action, p. 556; p. 559

What is needed for a sound expansion of production is additional capital goods, not money or fiduciary media. The credit boom is built on the sands of banknotes and deposits. It must collapse.

Human Action, p. 559; p. 561

If the credit expansion is not stopped in time, the boom turns into the crack-up boom; the flight into real values begins, and the whole monetary system founders.

Human Action, p. 559; p. 562

The final outcome of the credit expansion is general impoverishment.

Human Action, p. 562; p. 564

Credit expansion is the governments' foremost tool in their struggle against the market economy. In their hands it is the magic wand designed to conjure away the scarcity of capital goods, to lower the rate of interest or to abolish it altogether, to finance lavish government spending, to expropriate the capitalists, to contrive everlasting booms, and to make everybody prosperous.

Human Action, p. 788; p. 794

CREDITORS

Every grant of credit is a speculative entrepreneurial venture, the success or failure of which is uncertain.

Human Action, p. 536; p. 539

Over all species of deferred payments hangs, like the sword of Damocles, the danger of government interference. Public opinion has always been biased against creditors.

Human Action, p. 537; p. 540

Lenders of money have been held in odium, at all times and among all peoples.

The Theory of Money and Credit, p. 264

CULTURE

After all, culture is wealth. Without well-being, without wealth, there never has been culture.

Nation, State, and Economy, p. 74

They strive for welfare and for wealth not because they see the highest value in them but because they know that all higher and inner culture presupposes outward welfare.

Nation, State, and Economy, p. 215

We owe the origin and development of human society and, consequently, of culture and civilization, to the fact that work performed under the division of labor is more productive than when performed in isolation.

Epistemological Problems of Economics, p. 110

A higher standard of living also brings about a higher standard of culture and civilization.

Economic Policy, p. 89

DEATH

Man lives in the shadow of death. Whatever he may have achieved in the course of his pilgrimage, he must one day pass away and abandon all that he has built. Each instant can become his last. There is only one thing that is certain about the individual's future—death.

Human Action, p. 877; p. 881

True, man cannot escape death. But for the present he is alive; and life, not death, takes hold of him. Whatever the future may have in store for him, he cannot withdraw from the necessities of the actual hour. As long as a man lives, he cannot help obeying the cardinal impulse, the *elan vital.* It is man's innate nature that he seeks to preserve and to strengthen his life, that he is discontented and aims at removing uneasiness, that he is in search of what may be called happiness.

Human Action, pp. 877–78; pp. 881–82

DEFICITS

A policy of deficit spending saps the very foundation of all interpersonal relations and contracts. It frustrates all kinds of savings, social security benefits and pensions.

Planning for Freedom, p. 89

It is always an inflationist policy, not "economic conditions," which bring about the monetary depreciation. The evil is philosophical in character.

On the Manipulation of Money and Credit, p. 48

If one regards inflation as an evil, then one has to stop inflating. One has to balance the budget of the government.

Economic Policy, pp. 72–73

If the practice persists of covering government deficits with the issue of notes, then the day will come without fail, sooner or later, when the monetary systems of those nations pursuing this course will break down completely. The purchasing power of the monetary unit will decline more and more, until finally it disappears completely.

On the Manipulation of Money and Credit, p. 5

Can anyone doubt that the warring people of Europe would have tired of the conflict much sooner, if their governments had clearly, candidly, and promptly, presented them with the bill for military expenses?

On the Manipulation of Money and Credit, p. 38

In public administration there is no connection between revenue and expenditure.

Bureaucracy, p. 47

What the doctrine of balancing budgets over a period of many years really means is this: As long as our own party is in office, we will enhance our popularity by reckless spending. We do not want to annoy our friends by cutting down expenditure. We want the voters to feel happy under the artificial short-lived prosperity which the easy money policy and rich supply of additional money generate. Later, when our adversaries will be in office, the inevitable consequence of our expansionist policy, viz., depression, will appear. Then we shall blame them for the disaster and assail them for their failure to balance the budget properly.

Planning for Freedom, p. 87

The two pillars of democratic government are the primacy of the law and the budget.

Bureaucracy, p. 41

If it is unnecessary to adjust the amount of expenditure to the means available, there is no limit to the spending of the great god State.

Planning for Freedom, p. 90

What the government spends more, the public spends less. Public works are not accomplished by the miraculous power of a magic wand. They are paid for by funds taken away from the citizens.

Human Action, p. 655; p. 659

DEMOCRACY

Democracy is not a good that people can enjoy without trouble. It is, on the contrary, a treasure that must be daily defended and conquered anew by strenuous effort.

Bureaucracy, p. 121

Democracy too is not divine.

Omnipotent Government, p. 47

Majorities are no less exposed to error and frustration than kings and dictators. That a fact is deemed true by the majority does not prove its truth. That a policy is deemed expedient by the majority does not prove its expediency. The individuals who form the majority are not gods, and their joint conclusions are not necessarily godlike.

Omnipotent Government, p. 47

People can today seek salvation only in democracy, in the right of self-determination both of individuals and of nations.

Nation, State, and Economy, p. 131

DEVELOPMENT

What is lacking to the underdeveloped nations is not knowledge, but capital.

The Ultimate Foundation of Economic Science, p. 127

The prerequisite for more economic equality in the world is industrialization. And this is possible only through increased capital investment, increased capital accumulation.

Economic Policy, p. 86

The poverty of the backward nations is due to the fact that their policies of expropriation, discriminatory taxation and foreign exchange control prevent the investment of foreign capital while their domestic policies preclude the accumulation of indigenous capital.

The Anti-Capitalistic Mentality, p. 83

What is called the American way of life is the result of the fact that the United States has put fewer obstacles in the way of saving and capital accumulation than in other nations. The economic backwardness of such countries as India consists precisely in the fact that their policies hinder both the accumulation of domestic capital and the investment of foreign capital. As the capital required is lacking, the Indian enterprises are prevented from employing sufficient quantities of modern equipment, are therefore producing much less per man-hour and can only afford to pay wage rates which, compared with American wage rates, appear as shockingly low.

Planning for Freedom, p. 152

It is not true that the economic backwardness of foreign countries is to be imputed to technological ignorance on the part of their peoples.

Planning for Freedom, p. 196

It is not a lack of the "know how" that prevents foreign countries from fully adopting American methods of manufacturing, but the insufficiency of capital available.

Planning for Freedom, p. 197

Capitalists have the tendency to move towards those countries in which there is plenty of labor available and in which labor is reasonable. And by the fact that they bring capital into these countries, they bring about a trend toward higher wage rates.

Economic Policy, p. 89

DICTATORSHIP

Most of the tyrants, despots, and dictators are sincerely convinced that their rule is beneficial for the people, that theirs is government *for the people.*

Bureaucracy, p. 43

Every dictator plans to rear, raise, feed, and train his fellow men as the breeder does his cattle. His aim is not to make the people happy but to bring them into a condition which renders him, the dictator, happy. He wants to domesticate them, to give them cattle status. The cattle breeder also is a benevolent despot.

Bureaucracy, p. 91

Nobody every recommended a dictatorship aiming at ends other than those he himself approved. He who advocates dictatorship always advocates the unrestricted rule of his own will.

Omnipotent Government, p. 242

DISCLOSURE

Governments and local administrative bodies decide to inform the public of their mistakes only when losses have become disproportionately great.

Epistemological Problems of Economics, p. 226

DISCRIMINATION

Like the mystical sense of communion, racial hatred is not a natural phenomenon innate in man. It is a product of ideologies.

Human Action, p. 168; p. 168

An employer or an employee entrusted with the management of a department of an enterprise is free to discriminate in hiring workers, to fire them arbitrarily, or to cut down their wages below the market rate. But in indulging in such arbitrary acts he jeopardizes the profitability of his enterprise or his department and thereby impairs his own income and his position in the economic system.

Human Action, p. 629; p. 634

True, the entrepreneur is free to give full rein to his whims, to dismiss workers off hand, to cling stubbornly to antiquated processes, deliberately to choose unsuitable methods of production and to allow himself to be guided by motives which conflict with the demands of consumers. But when and in so far as he does this he must pay for it, and if he does not restrain himself in time he will be driven, by the loss of his property, into a position where he can inflict no further damage. Special means of controlling his behavior are unnecessary. The market controls him more strictly and exactingly than could any government or other organ of society.

Socialism, p. 401

DIVISION OF LABOR

Within the framework of social cooperation every citizen depends on the services rendered by all his fellow citizens.

Bureaucracy, p. 77

Under the division of labor, the structure of society rests on the shoulders of all men and women.

Bureaucracy, pp. 77–78

Every expansion of the personal division of labor brings advantages to all who take part in it.

Socialism, p. 261

The greater productivity of work under the division of labor is a unifying influence. It leads men to regard each other as comrades in a joint struggle for welfare, rather than as competitors in a struggle for existence. It makes friends out of enemies, peace out of war, society out of individuals.

Socialism, p. 261

Originally confined to the narrowest circles of people, to immediate neighbors, the division of labor gradually becomes more general until eventually it includes all mankind.

Socialism, p. 279

Now the greatest accomplishment of reason is the discovery of the advantages of social cooperation, and its corollary, the division of labor.

Omnipotent Government, p. 121

Economic history is the development of the division of labor.

Nation, State, and Economy, p. 134

It is by virtue of the division of labor that man is distinguished from the animals. It is the division of labor that has made feeble man, far inferior to most animals in physical strength, the lord of the earth and the creator of the marvels of technology.

Liberalism, p. 18

DRUGS

The alcoholic and the drug addict harm only themselves by their behavior; the person who violates the rules of morality governing man's life in society harms not only himself, but everyone.

Liberalism, p. 35

As soon as we surrender the principle that the state should not interfere in any questions touching on the individual's mode of life, we end by regulating and restricting the latter down to the smallest details.

Liberalism, p. 54

Let no one object that the struggle against morphinism and the struggle against "evil" literature are two quite different things. The only difference between them is that some of the same people who favor the prohibition of the former will not agree to the prohibition of the latter.

Liberalism, p. 54

It is an established fact that alcoholism, cocainism, and morphinism are deadly enemies of life, of health, and of the capacity for work and enjoyment; and a utilitarian must therefore consider them as vices. But this is far from demonstrating that the authorities must interpose to suppress these vices by commercial prohibitions, nor is it by any means evident that such intervention on the part of a government is really capable of suppressing them or that, even if this end could be attained, it might not therewith open up a Pandora's box of other dangers, no less mischievous than alcoholism and morphinism. . . . For if the majority of citizens is, in principle, conceded the right to impose its way of life upon a minority, it is impossible to stop at prohibitions against indulgences, in alcohol, morphine, and cocaine, and similar poisons. Why should not what is valid for these poisons be valid also for nicotine, caffeine, and the like? Why should not the state generally prescribe which foods may be indulged in and which must be avoided because they are injurious? . . . More harmful still than all these pleasures, many will say, is the reading of evil literature.

Liberalism, p. 53

ECONOMETRICS

As a method of economic analysis econometrics is a childish play with figures that does not contribute anything to the elucidation of the problems of economic reality.

The Ultimate Foundation of Economic Science, p. 63

The specific experience with which economics and economic statistics are concerned always refers to the past. It is history, and as such does not provide knowledge about a regularity that will manifest itself also in the future.

Epistemological Problems of Economics, p. xiv

As there are in the field of social affairs no constant relations between magnitudes, no measurement is possible and economics can never become quantitative.

The Theory of Money and Credit, p. 460

Every quantity that we can observe is a historical event, a fact which cannot be fully described without specifying the time and geographical point. The econometrician is unable to disprove this fact, which cuts the ground from under his reasoning. He cannot help admitting that there are no "behavior constants." Nonetheless he wants to introduce some numbers, arbitrarily chosen on the basis of a historical fact, as "unknown *behavior constants.*"

Theory and History, p. 10

ECONOMIC CALCULATION

What economic calculation requires is a monetary system whose functioning is not sabotaged by government interference.

Human Action, p. 225; pp. 223–24

The endeavors to expand the quantity of money in circulation either in order to increase the government's capacity to spend or in order to bring about a temporary lowering of the rate of interest disintegrate all currency matters and derange economic calculation.

Human Action, p. 225; p. 224

Admittedly, monetary calculation has its inconveniences and serious defects, but we have certainly nothing better to put in its place, and for the practical purposes of life monetary calculation as it exists under a sound monetary system always suffices. Were we to dispense with it, any economic system of calculation would become absolutely impossible.

Economic Calculation in the Socialist Commonwealth, p. 25

Economic calculation can only take place by means of money prices established in the market for production goods in a society resting on private property in the means of production.

Socialism, p. 123

Without the aid of monetary calculation, bookkeeping, and the computation of profit and loss in terms of money, technology would have had to confine itself to the simplest, and therefore the least productive, methods.

Epistemological Problems of Economics, p. 157

Monetary calculation is not the calculation, and certainly not the measurement, of value. Its basis is the comparison of the more important and the less important. It is an ordering according to rank, an act of grading, and not an act of measuring.

Epistemological Problems of Economics, p. 160

ECONOMIC DEVELOPMENT

The problem of rendering the underdeveloped nations more prosperous cannot be solved by material aid. It is a spiritual and intellectual problem. Prosperity is not simply a matter of capital investment. It is an ideological issue. What the underdeveloped countries need first is the ideology of economic freedom and private enterprise.

Money, Method, and the Market Process, p. 173

ECONOMIC PROGRESS

Economic progress is the work of the savers, who accumulate capital, and of the entrepreneurs, who turn capital to new uses. The other members of society, of course, enjoy the advantages of progress, but they not only do not contribute anything to it; they even place obstacles in its way.

Epistemological Problems of Economics, p. 228

ECONOMICS

Economics is not about goods and services; it is about human choice and action.

Human Action, p. 491; p. 494

Economics deals with real man, weak and subject to error as he is, not with ideal beings, omniscient and perfect as only gods could be.

Human Action, p. 97; p. 97

Economics must not be relegated to classrooms and statistical offices and must not be left to esoteric circles. It is the philosophy of human life and action and concerns everybody and everything. It is the pith of civilization and of man's human existence.

Human Action, p. 874; p. 878

The economist must never be a specialist. In dealing with any problem he must always fix his glance upon the whole system.

Austrian Economics: An Anthology, p. 157

Despots and democratic majorities are drunk with power. They must reluctantly admit that they are subject to the laws of nature. But they reject the very notion of economic law . . . economic history is a long record of government policies that failed because they were designed with a bold disregard for the laws of economics.

Austrian Economics: An Anthology, p. 155

Economics as such is a challenge to the conceit of those in power. An economist can never be a favorite of autocrats and demagogues. With them he is always the mischief-maker, and the more they are inwardly convinced that his objections are well founded, the more they hate him.

Austrian Economics: An Anthology, p. 155

There is economics and there is economic history. The two must never be confused.

Austrian Economics: An Anthology p. 155

The unpopularity of economics is the result of its analysis of the effects of privileges. It is impossible to invalidate the economists' demonstration that all privileges hurt the interests of the rest of the nation or at least a great part of it.

Austrian Economics: An Anthology, p. 58

The social function of economic science consists precisely in developing sound economic theories and in exploding the fallacies of vicious reasoning. In the pursuit of this task the economist incurs the deadly enmity of all mountebanks and charlatans whose shortcuts to an earthly paradise he debunks.

Economic Freedom and Interventionism, pp. 51–52

All those not familiar with economics (i.e., the immense majority) do not see any reason why they should not coerce other people by means of force to do what these people are not prepared to do of their own accord.

Austrian Economics: An Anthology, p. 75

The main achievement of economics is that it has provided a theory of peaceful human cooperation. This is why the harbingers of violent conflict have branded it as a "dismal science" and why this age of wars, civil wars, and destruction has no use for it.

Economic Freedom and Interventionism, p. 235

No very deep knowledge of economics is usually needed for grasping the immediate effects of a measure; but the task of economics is to foretell the remoter effects, and so to allow us to avoid such acts as attempt to remedy a present ill by sowing the seeds of a much greater ill for the future.

The Theory of Money and Credit, p. 23

This dilettantish inability to comprehend the essential issues of the conduct of production affairs is not only manifested in the writings of Marx and Engels. It permeates no less the contributions of contemporary pseudo-economics.

Planning for Freedom, p. 147

But for a few dozen individuals all over the globe are cognizant of economics, and no statesman or politician cares about it.

A Critique of Interventionism, p. 106

Rulers do not like to admit that their power is restricted by any laws other than those of physics and biology. They never ascribe their failures and frustrations to the violation of economic law.

Human Action, p. 756; p. 762

The development of a profession of economists is an offshoot of interventionism. The professional economist is the specialist who is instrumental in designing various measures of government interference with business. He is an expert in the field of economic legislation, which today invariably aims at hindering the operation of the market economy.

Human Action, p. 865; p. 869

As conditions are today, nothing can be more important to every intelligent man than economics. His own fate and that of his progeny is at stake.

Human Action, p. 875; p. 878

Whether we like it or not, it is a fact that economics cannot remain an esoteric branch of knowledge accessible only to small groups of scholars and specialists. Economics deals with society's fundamental problems; it concerns everyone and belongs to all. It is the main and proper study of every citizen.

Human Action, p. 875; p. 879

The study of economics has been again and again led astray by the vain idea that economics must proceed according to the pattern of other sciences.

The Ultimate Foundation of Economic Science, p. 3

Economics is not specifically about business; it deals with all market phenomena and with all their aspects, not only with the activities of a businessman.

The Ultimate Foundation of Economic Science, p. 77

Everything that we say about action is independent of the motives that cause it and of the goals toward which it strives in the individual case. It makes no difference whether action springs from altruistic or from egoistic motives, from a noble or from a base disposition; whether it is directed toward the attainment of materialistic or idealistic ends; whether it arises from exhaustive and painstaking deliberation or follows fleeting impulses and passions.

Epistemological Problems of Economics, p. 34

Only by letting fall morsels of statistics is it possible for the economic theorist to maintain his prestige.

The Theory of Money and Credit, p. 216

People may disagree on the question of whether everybody ought to study economics seriously. But one thing is certain. A man who publicly talks or writes about the opposition between capitalism and socialism without having fully familiarized himself with all that economics has to say about these issues is an irresponsible babbler.

The Anti-Capitalistic Mentality, p. 47

In all ages the pioneer in scientific thought has been a solitary thinker. But never has the position of the scientist been more solitary than in the field of modern economics. The fate of mankind—progress on the road that western civilization has taken for thousands of years, or a rapid plunge into a chaos from which there is no way out, from which no new life as we know it will ever develop—depends on whether this condition persists.

Epistemological Problems of Economics, p. 202

The body of economic knowledge is an essential element in the structure of human civilization; it is the foundation upon which modern industrialism and all the moral, intellectual, technological, and therapeutical achievements of the last centuries have been built.

Human Action, p. 885

ECONOMISTS

There is, in fact, in the writings and teaching of those who nowadays call themselves "economists," no longer any comprehension of the operation of the economic system as such.

Economic Freedom and Interventionism, p. 154

In the same way in which it is impossible for a mathematician to specialize in triangles and to neglect the study of circles, it is impossible to be an expert on wage rates without at the same time mastering the problems of profits and interest, commodity prices, and currency and banking.

Economic Freedom and Interventionism, p. 234

There are only economists and laymen. There are no such things as labor economists or farm economists.

Economic Freedom and Interventionism, p. 234

EDUCATION

There is, in fact, only *one* solution: the state, the government, the laws must not in any way concern themselves with schooling or education. Public funds must not be used for such purposes. The rearing and instruction of youth must be left entirely to parents and to private associations and institutions.

Liberalism, p. 115

European totalitarianism is an upshot of bureaucracy's preeminence in the field of education. The universities paved the way for the dictators.

Bureaucracy, p. 87

The pseudo-liberals monopolize the teaching jobs at many universities. Only men who agree with them are appointed as teachers and instructors of the social sciences, and only textbooks supporting their ideas are used.

Planning for Freedom, p. 162

Tax-supported universities are under the sway of the party in power. The authorities try to appoint only professors who are ready to advance ideas of which they themselves approve.

Human Action, p. 868; p. 872

The majority of the students espouse without any inhibitions the interventionist panaceas recommended by their professors.

Human Action, p. 871; p. 875

What has made many of the present-day universities by and large nurseries of socialism is not so much the conditions prevailing in the departments of economics as the teachings handed down in other departments.

Human Action, p. 871; p. 875

What is wrong with the discipline that is nowadays taught in most universities under the misleading label of economics is not that the teachers and the authors of the textbooks are either not businessmen or failed in their business enterprises. The fault is with their ignorance of economics and with their inability to think logically.

The Ultimate Foundation of Economic Science, p. 78

Continued adherence to a policy of compulsory education is utterly incompatible with efforts to establish lasting peace.

Liberalism, p. 114

Western Europe developed the system of obligatory public education. It came to Eastern Europe as an achievement of Western civilization. But in the linguistically mixed territories it turned into a dreadful weapon in the hands of governments determined to change the linguistic allegiance of their subjects. The philanthropists and pedagogues of England who advocated public education did not foresee what waves of hatred and resentment would rise out of this institution.

Omnipotent Government, pp. 82–83

The modern American high school, reformed according to the principles of John Dewey, has failed lamentably, as all competent experts agree, in the teaching of mathematics, physics, languages, and history.

Economic Freedom and Interventionism, p. 171

Innovators and creative geniuses cannot be reared in schools. They are precisely the men who defy what the school has taught them.

Human Action, p. 311, p. 314

Education rears disciples, imitators, and routinists, not pioneers of new ideas and creative geniuses. . . . The mark of the creative mind is that it defies a part of what it has learned or, at least, adds something new to it.

Bureaucracy, p. 71

ELECTIONS

The horrors of revolution and civil war can be avoided if a disliked government can be smoothly dislodged at the next election.

The Historical Setting of the Austrian School, p. 35

ENTREPRENEUR

The planning businessman cannot help employing data concerning the unknown future; he deals with future prices and future costs of production.

Human Action, p. 225; p. 224

The entrepreneurs . . . are not infallible and often blunder. But they are less liable to error, and blunder less than other people do.

Planning for Freedom, p. 114

A technological invention is not something material. It is the product of a mental process, of reasoning and conceiving new ideas. The tools and machines may be called material, but the operation of the mind which created them is certainly spiritual.

Theory and History, p. 109

The only source from which an entrepreneur's profits stem is his ability to anticipate better than other people the future demand of the consumers.

Human Action, p. 288; p. 290

The task of the entrepreneur is to select from the multitude of technologically feasible projects those which will satisfy the most urgent of the not yet satisfied needs of the public.

Planning for Freedom, p. 117

What distinguishes the successful entrepreneur and promoter from other people is precisely the fact that he does not let himself be guided by what was and is, but arranges his affairs on the ground of his opinion about the future. He sees the past and the present as other people do; but he judges the future in a different way.

Human Action, p. 582; p. 585

No dullness and clumsiness on the part of the masses can stop the pioneers of improvement. There is no need for them to win the approval of inert people beforehand. They are free to embark upon their projects even if everyone else laughs at them.

Human Action, p. 859; p. 863

In order to succeed in business a man does not need a degree from a school of business administration. These schools train the subalterns for routine jobs. They certainly do not train entrepreneurs. An entrepreneur cannot be trained. A man becomes an entrepreneur by seizing an opportunity and filling the gap. No special education is required for such a display of keen judgment, foresight, and energy.

Human Action, p. 311, p. 314

ENVIRONMENT

Animals are forced to adjust themselves to the natural conditions of their environment; if they do not succeed in this process of adjustment, they are wiped out. Man is the only animal that is able—within definite limits—to adjust his environment purposively to suit him better.

The Ultimate Foundation of Economic Science, p. 8

It is vain to provide for the needs of ages the technological abilities of which we cannot even dream.

Human Action, p. 383; p. 386

Talk about the magnificence of untouched nature is idle if it does not take into account what man has got by "desecrating" nature. The earth's marvels were certainly splendid when visitors seldom set foot upon them. Commercially organized tourist traffic made them accessible to the many. The man who thinks "What a pity not to be alone on this peak! Intruders spoil my pleasure," fails to remember that he himself probably would not be on the spot if business had not provided all the facilities required. The technique of the historicists' indictment of capitalism is simple indeed. They take all its achievements for granted, but blame it for the disappearance of some enjoyments that are incompatible with it and for some imperfections which still may disfigure its products. They forget that mankind has had to pay a price for its achievements—a price paid willingly because people believe that the gain derived, e.g., the prolongation of the average length of life, is more to be desired.

Theory and History, pp. 218–19

ENVY

The masses do not like those who surpass them in any regard. The average man envies and hates those who are different.

The Ultimate Foundation of Economic Science, p. 123

What pushes the masses into the camp of socialism is, even more than the illusion that socialism will make them richer, the expectation that it will curb all those who are better than they themselves are. . . . There will no longer be any room left for innovators and reformers.

The Ultimate Foundation of Economic Science, p. 123

Nobody seems to doubt that to prevent some people from acquiring riches is a policy extremely beneficial for the rest of society. Everybody is sincerely convinced that technological progress is an act of God not conditioned by the methods of social organization. Enjoying all the new products which free enterprise provides, they are tormented by one thought only: that some people have become rich in creating these new things.

Economic Freedom and Interventionism, pp. 231–32

EQUALITY

Nothing, however, is as ill founded as the assertion of the alleged equality of all members of the human race.

Liberalism, p. 28

Collaboration of the more talented, more able, and more industrious with the less talented, less able, and less industrious results in benefit for both. The gains derived from the division of labor are always mutual.

Human Action, p. 159; p. 160

The heir of a wealthy man [undoubtedly] enjoys a certain advantage as he starts under more favorable conditions than others.

The Anti-Capitalistic Mentality, pp. 40–41

The egalitarian doctrine is manifestly contrary to all the facts established by biology and by history. Only fanatical partisans of this theory can contend that what distinguishes the genius from the dullard is entirely the effect of postnatal influences.

Theory and History, p. 331

We cannot really say any more about the inherited characteristics of the individual than that some men are more gifted from birth than others. Where the difference between good and bad is to be sought we cannot say.

Socialism, p. 288

Men are unequal; individuals differ from one another. They differ because their prenatal as well as their postnatal history is never identical.

The Ultimate Foundation of Economic Science, p. 59

Equality of opportunity is a factor neither in prize fights and beauty contests nor in any other field of competition, whether biological or social. The immense majority of people are by the physiological structure of their bodies deprived of a chance to attain the honors of a boxing champion or a beauty queen. Only very few people can compete on the labor market as opera singers and movie stars.

Human Action, p. 276; p. 276

In talking about equality and asking vehemently for its realization, nobody advocates a curtailment of his own present income.

Planning for Freedom, p. 137

What those people who ask for equality have in mind is always an increase in their own power to consume.

Human Action, p. 836; p. 840

The idea of equal distribution of land is a pernicious illusion. Its execution would plunge mankind into misery and starvation, and would in fact wipe out civilization itself.

Theory and History, p. 354

EQUILIBRIUM

It is only the passionate pro-socialist zeal of mathematical pseudo-economists that transforms a purely analytical tool of logical economics into an utopian image of the good and most desirable state of affairs.

Theory and History, p. 367

EUROPE

If the goal of the Pan-European movement could be achieved, the world would not be in the least the better for it. The struggle of a united European continent against the great world powers outside its territory would be no less ruinous than is the present struggle of the countries of Europe among themselves.

Liberalism, p. 147

If one wants to study the reasons for Europe's backwardness, it would be necessary to examine the manifold laws and regulations that prevented in Europe the establishment of an equivalent of the American drug store and crippled the evolution of chain stores, department stores, super markets and kindred outfits.

Planning for Freedom, p. 136

One cannot counteract the policy of economic isolation on a national scale by replacing it with the same policy on the part of a larger political entity comprising a number of different nationalities. The only way to counteract tendencies toward protectionism and autarky is to recognize their harmfulness and to appreciate the harmony of the interests of all nations.

Liberalism, pp. 146–47

EXCHANGE

All human action, so far as it is rational, appears as the exchange of one condition for another. Men apply economic goods and personal time and labour in the direction which, under the given circumstances, promises the highest degree of satisfaction, and they forgo the satisfaction of lesser needs so as to satisfy the more urgent needs. This is the essence of economic activity—the carrying out of acts of exchange.

Socialism, p. 97

Each party attaches a higher value to the good he receives than to that he gives away. The exchange ratio, the price, is not the product of an equality of valuation, but, on the contrary, the product of a discrepancy in valuation.

Human Action, pp. 328–29; p. 331

There are in the market economy no conflicts between the interests of the buyers and sellers.

Human Action, p. 661; p. 665

The deal is always advantageous both for the buyer and the seller. Even a man who sells at a loss is still better off than he would be if he could not sell at all, or only at a still lower price. He loses on account of his lack of foresight; the sale limits his loss even if the price received is low. If both the buyer and the seller were not to consider the transaction as the most advantageous action they could choose under the prevailing conditions, they would not enter into the deal.

Human Action, pp. 661–62; pp. 665–66

He [a consumer] buys because he believes that to acquire the merchandise in question will satisfy him better than keeping the money or spending it for something else.

The Ultimate Foundation of Economic Science, p. 76

In a game there are winners and losers. But a business deal is always advantageous for both parties. If both the buyer and the seller were not to consider the transaction as the most advantageous action they could choose under the prevailing conditions, they would not enter into the deal.

The Ultimate Foundation of Economic Science, p. 90

The valuation of a monetary unit depends *not* on the wealth of a country, but rather on the relationship between the quantity of, and demand for, money. Thus, even the richest country can have a bad currency and the poorest a good one.

On the Manipulation of Money and Credit, p. 21

EXPECTATIONS

There is neither constancy nor continuity in the valuations and in the formation of exchange ratios between various commodities. Every new datum brings about a reshuffling of the whole price structure. Understanding, by trying to grasp what is going on in the minds of the men concerned, can approach the problem of forecasting future conditions. We may call its methods unsatisfactory and the positivists may arrogantly scorn it. But such arbitrary judgments must not and cannot obscure the fact that understanding is the only appropriate method of dealing with the uncertainty of future conditions.

Human Action, p. 118; p. 118

EXPERIENCE

Experience is a mental act on the part of thinking and acting men.

The Ultimate Foundation of Economic Science, p. 15

Experience tells us something we did not know before and could not learn but for having had the experience.

The Ultimate Foundation of Economic Science, p. 18

No thinking and no acting would be possible to man if the universe were chaotic, i.e., if there were no regularity whatever in the succession and concatenation of events. In such a world of unlimited contingency. . . . There would be no possibility for man to expect anything. All experience would be merely historical, the record of what has happened in the past. No inference from past events to what might happen in the future would be permissible.

The Ultimate Foundation of Economic Science, pp. 19–20

New experience can force us to discard or modify inferences we have drawn from previous experience.

Epistemological Problems of Economics, p. 27

FAIRNESS

The concept of a "just" or "fair" price is devoid of any scientific meaning; it is a disguise for wishes, a striving for a state of affairs different from reality.

Human Action, p. 329; p. 332

There is no such thing as a just and fair method of exercising the tremendous power that interventionism puts into the hands of the legislature and the executive. The advocates of interventionism pretend to substitute for the—as they assert, "socially" detrimental—effects of private property and vested interests the unlimited discretion of the perfectly wise and disinterested legislator and his conscientious and indefatigable servants, the bureaucrats.

Human Action, No Entry; pp. 734–35

To the grumbler who complains about the unfairness of the market system only one piece of advice can be given: If you want to acquire wealth, then try to satisfy the public by offering them something that is cheaper or which they like better. Try to supersede Pinkapinka by mixing another beverage. Equality under the law gives you the power to challenge every millionaire. It is—in a market not sabotaged by government-imposed restrictions—exclusively your fault if you do not outstrip the chocolate king, the movie star and the boxing champion.

The Anti-Capitalistic Mentality, pp. 9–10.

Daydreams of a "fair" world which would treat him according to his "real worth" are the refuge of all those plagued by a lack of self-knowledge.

The Anti-Capitalistic Mentality, p. 15

FARM PROGRAMS

It is not in the power of the government to make everybody more prosperous. It can raise the income of the farmers by forcibly restricting domestic agricultural production. But the higher prices of farm products are paid by the consumers, not by the state. The counterpart of the farmers' higher standard of living is the lowering of the standard of living of the rest of the nation.

Bureaucracy, p. 84

The boon of these privileged farmers is paid for by the taxpayers who must provide the funds required to defray the deficit. It affects neither the market price nor the total available supply of agricultural products. It merely makes profitable the operation of farms which hitherto were submarginal and makes other farms, the operation of which was hitherto profitable, submarginal.

Human Action, p. 656; p. 660

It is true that there is such a thing as the *corn-hog cycle* and analogous happenings in the production of other farm products. But the recurrence of such cycles is due to the fact that the penalties which the market applies against inefficient and clumsy entrepreneurs do not affect a great part of the farmers. These farmers are not answerable for their actions because they are the pet children of governments and politicians. If it were not so, they would long since have gone bankrupt and their former farms would be operated by more intelligent people.

Human Action, p. 583; p. 586

FATE

If Dante, Shakespeare, or Beethoven had died in childhood, mankind would miss what it owes to them. In this sense we may say that chance plays a role in human affairs.

The Ultimate Foundation of Economic Science, p. 61

There always remains an orbit that to the limited knowledge of man appears as an orbit of pure chance and marks life as a gamble. Man and his works are always exposed to the impact of unforeseen and uncontrollable events.

The Ultimate Foundation of Economic Science, pp. 65–66

Even knowledge of the laws of nature does not make action free. It is never able to attain more than definite, limited ends. It can never go beyond the insurmountable barriers set for it. And even within the sphere allowed to it, it must always reckon with the inroads of uncontrollable forces, with fate.

Epistemological Problems of Economics, p. 198

Fatalism is so contrary to human nature that few people were prepared to draw all the conclusions to which it leads and to adjust their conduct accordingly. It is a fable that the victories of the Arabian conquerors in the first centuries of Islam were due to the fatalist teachings of Mohammed. The leaders of the Moslem armies which within an unbelievably short time conquered a great part of the Mediterranean area did not put a fatalistic confidence in Allah. Rather they believed that their God was for the big, well-equipped, and skillfully led battalions. . . . Nor was the lethargy which spread later among the Islamitic peoples caused by the fatalism of their religion. It was despotism that paralyzed the initiative of the subjects. The harsh tyrants who oppressed the masses were certainly not lethargic and apathetic. They were indefatigable in their quest for power, riches, and pleasures.

Theory and History, pp. 79–80

FEDERALISM

Seen from the formalistic viewpoint of constitutional law, the United States and the Swiss Confederation may doubtless still be classified as federations, but in actual fact they are moving more and more toward centralization.

Omnipotent Government, p. 268

FEMINISM

So far as Feminism seeks to adjust the legal position of woman to that of man, so far as it seeks to offer her legal and economic freedom to develop and act in accordance with her inclinations, desires, and economic circumstances—so far it is nothing more than a branch of the great liberal movement, which advocates peaceful and free evolution. When, going beyond this, it attacks the institutions of social life under the impression that it will thus be able to remove the natural barriers, it is a spiritual child of Socialism. For it is a characteristic of Socialism to discover in social institutions the origin of unalterable facts of nature, and to endeavor, by reforming these institutions, to reform nature.

Socialism, p. 87

Woman's struggle to preserve her personality in marriage is part of that struggle for personal integrity which characterizes the rationalist society of the economic order based on private ownership of the means of production. It is not exclusively to the interest of woman that she should succeed in this struggle; to contrast the interests of men and women, as extreme feminists try to do, is very foolish. All mankind would suffer if woman should fail to develop her ego and be unable to unite with man as equal, freeborn companions and comrades.

Socialism, pp. 90–91

FIAT MONEY

For the naive mind there is something miraculous in the issuance of fiat money. A magic word spoken by the government creates out of nothing a thing which can be exchanged against any merchandise a man would like to get. How pale is the art of sorcerers, witches, and conjurors when compared with that of the government's Treasury Department!

The Theory of Money and Credit, p. 458

FISHER, IRVING

Thus we are in a position to see that Fisher's proposal actually offers no more than was offered by any previous plan for a multiple standard. In regard to the role of money as a standard of deferred payments, the verdict must be that, for long-term contracts, Fisher's scheme is inadequate. For short-term commitments, it is both inadequate and superfluous.

On the Manipulation of Money and Credit, p. 95

FOREIGN AID

The worst method to fight communism is that of the Marshall Plan. . . . The United States, they think, is aiding them because its people have a bad conscience. They themselves pocket this bribe but their sympathies go to the socialist system. The American subsidies make it possible for their governments to conceal partially the disastrous effects of the various socialist measures they have adopted.

Planning for Freedom, pp. 141–42

We must comprehend that it is impossible to improve the economic conditions of the underdeveloped nations by grants in aid. If we send them foodstuffs to fight famines, we merely relieve their governments from the necessity of abandoning their disastrous agricultural policies.

Money, Method, and the Market Process, p. 172

The truth is that the United States is subsidizing all over the world the worst failure of history: socialism. But for these lavish subsidies the continuation of the socialist schemes would have become long since unfeasible.

Money, Method, and the Market Process, p. 173

FOREIGN CAPITAL

Capitalists have the tendency to move towards those countries in which there is plenty of labor available and at which labor is reasonable. And by the fact that they bring capital into these countries, they bring about a trend toward higher wage rates.

Economic Policy, p. 89

The enormous transfer of capital from Western Europe to the rest of the world was one of the outstanding events of the age of capitalism. It has developed natural resources in the remotest areas. It has raised the standard of living of peoples who from time immemorial had not achieved any improvement in their material conditions.

Omnipotent Government, p. 102

With the end of a great period in the nineteenth century when foreign capital helped to develop, in all parts of the world, modern methods of transportation, manufacturing, mining, and agriculture, there came a new era in which the governments and the political parties considered the foreign investor as an *exploiter* who should be expelled from the country.

Economic Policy, p. 82

There has been much talk about the alleged exploitation of the debtor nations by the creditor nations. But if the concept of exploitation is to be applied to these relations, it is rather an exploitation of the investing by the receiving nations. These loans and investments were not intended as gifts. The loans were made upon solemn stipulation of payment of principal and interest. The investments were made in the expectation that property rights would be respected.

Omnipotent Government, p. 102

This throttling of international credit can hardly be remedied otherwise than by setting aside the principle that it lies within the discretion of every government . . . to stop paying interest to foreign countries and also to prohibit interest and amortization payments on the part of its subjects.

The Theory of Money and Credit, pp. 28–29

FOREIGN EXCHANGE

Foreign-exchange control is today primarily a device for the virtual expropriation of foreign investments. It has destroyed the international capital and money market. It is the main instrument of policies aiming at the elimination of imports and thereby at the economic isolation of the various countries. It is thus one of the most important factors in the decline of Western civilization.

The Theory of Money and Credit, p. 476

FREE MARKET

There is no kind of freedom and liberty other than the kind which the market economy brings about. In a totalitarian hegemonic society the only freedom that is left to the individual, because it cannot be denied to him, is the freedom to commit suicide.

Human Action, p. 280; p. 283

What gives to the individuals as much freedom as is compatible with life in society is the operation of the market economy. The constitutions and bills of rights do not create freedom. They merely protect the freedom that the competitive economic system grants to the individuals against encroachments on the part of the police power.

The Anti-Capitalistic Mentality, pp. 99–100

The market is a democracy in which every penny gives a right to vote. It is true that the various individuals have not the same power to vote. The richer man casts more ballots than the poorer fellow. But to be rich and to earn a higher income is, in the market economy, already the outcome of the previous election. The only means to acquire wealth and to preserve it, in a market economy not adulterated by government-made privileges and restrictions, is to serve the consumers in the best and cheapest way. Capitalists and landowners who fail in this regard suffer losses. If they do not change their procedure, they lose their wealth and become poor. It is the consumers who make poor people rich and rich people poor.

Planned Chaos, pp. 25–26

The market economy safeguards peaceful economic cooperation because it does not use force upon the economic plans of the citizens. If one masterplan is to be substituted for the plans of each citizen, endless fighting must emerge. Those who disagree with the dictator's plan have no other means to carry on than to defeat the despot by force of arms.

Planned Chaos, p. 30

The market economy is the social system of the division of labor under private ownership of the means of production. Everybody acts on his own behalf; but everybody's actions aim at the satisfaction of other people's needs as well as at the satisfaction of his own. Everybody in acting serves his fellow citizens. Everybody, on the other hand, is served by his fellow citizens. Everybody is both a means and an end in himself, an ultimate end for himself and a means to other people in their endeavors to attain their own ends.

Human Action, p. 258; p. 257

Liberty and freedom are the conditions of man within a contractual society.

Human Action, p. 280; p. 282

The market steers the capitalistic economy. It directs each individual's activities into those channels in which he best serves the wants of his fellow-men. The market alone puts the whole social system of private ownership of the means of production and free enterprise in order and provides it with sense and meaning.

Planning for Freedom, p. 72

The democracy of the market consists in the fact that people themselves make their choices and that no dictator has the power to force them to submit to his value judgments.

Human Action, p. 384; p. 387

Every step a government takes beyond the fulfillment of its essential function of protecting the smooth operation of the market economy against aggression, whether on the part of domestic or foreign disturbers, is a step forward on the road that directly leads into the totalitarian system where there is no freedom at all.

Human Action, No Entry; p. 282

The market economy [capitalism] was not devised by a master mind; it was not first planned as an utopian scheme and then put to work. Spontaneous actions of individuals, aiming at nothing else than at the improvement of their own state of satisfaction, undermined the prestige of the coercive status system step by step.

The Ultimate Foundation of Economic Science, p. 109

FREE TRADE

Free trade begins at home.

Omnipotent Government, p. 237

In our age of international division of labor, free trade is the prerequisite for any amicable arrangement between nations.

Omnipotent Government, p. 6

History is a struggle between two principles, the peaceful principle, which advances the development of trade, and the militarist-imperialist principle, which interprets human society not as a friendly division of labour but as the forcible repression of some of its members by others.

Socialism, p. 268

The nationalists stress the point that there is an irreconcilable conflict between the interests of various nations, but that, on the other hand, the rightly understood interests of all the citizens within the nation are harmonious. A nation can prosper only at the expense of other nations; the individual citizen can fare well only if his nation flourishes. The liberals have a different opinion. They believe that the interests of various nations harmonize no less than those of the various groups, classes, and strata of individuals within a nation. They believe that peaceful international cooperation is a more appropriate means than conflict for the attainment of the end which they and the nationalists are both aiming at: their own nation's welfare. They do not, as the nationalists charge, advocate peace and free trade in order to betray their own nation's interests to those of foreigners. On the contrary, they consider peace and free trade the best means to make their own nation wealthy. What separates the free traders from the nationalists are not ends, but the means recommended for attainment of the ends common to both.

Human Action, p. 183; p. 183

If trade were completely free, production would only take place under the most suitable conditions.

Socialism, p. 201

It is inconsistent to support a policy of low trade barriers. Either trade barriers are useful, then they cannot be high enough; or they are harmful, then they have to disappear completely.

Money, Method, and the Market Process, pp. 135–36

It is hopeless to expect a change by an international agreement. If a country thinks that more free trade is to its own advantage, then it may always open its frontiers.

Money, Method, and the Market Process, p. 136

FREEDOM

The distinction between an economic sphere of human life and activity and a noneconomic sphere is the worst of their fallacies. If an omnipotent authority has the power to assign to every individual the tasks he has to perform, nothing that can be called freedom and autonomy is left to him. He has only the choice between strict obedience and death by starvation.

Theory and History, pp. 376–77

Freedom must be granted to all, even to base people, lest the few who can use it for the benefit of mankind be hindered.

The Anti-Capitalistic Mentality, p. 108

As soon as the economic freedom which the market economy grants to its members is removed, all political liberties and bills of rights become humbug.

Human Action, p. 284; p. 287

Freedom is indivisible. As soon as one starts to restrict it, one enters upon a decline on which it is difficult to stop.

Human Action, p. 319; p. 322

The idea that political freedom can be preserved in the absence of economic freedom, and vice versa, is an illusion. Political freedom is the corollary of economic freedom.

Planning for Freedom, p. 38

The characteristic feature of a free society is that it can function in spite of the fact that its members disagree in many judgments of value.

Theory and History, p. 61

Freedom in society means that a man depends as much upon other people as other people depend on him.

Economic Policy, p. 19

Freedom really means *the freedom to make mistakes*.

Economic Policy, p. 22

Many of our contemporaries are firmly convinced that what is needed to render all human affairs perfectly satisfactory is brutal suppression of all "bad" people, i.e., of those with whom they disagree. They dream of a perfect system of government that—as they think—would have already long since been realized if these "bad" men, guided by stupidity and selfishness, had not hindered its establishment.

The Ultimate Foundation of Economic Science, p. 95

This, then, is freedom in the external life of man—that he is independent of the arbitrary power of his fellows. Such freedom is no natural right. It did not exist under primitive conditions. It arose in the process of social development and its final completion is the work of mature Capitalism.

Socialism, p. 171

When men have gained freedom in purely economic relationships they begin to desire it elsewhere.

Socialism, p. 171

The only true national autonomy is the freedom of the individual against the state and society.

Nation, State, and Economy, p. 96

As soon as we surrender the principle that the state should not interfere in any questions touching on the individual's mode of life, we end by regulating and restricting the latter down to the smallest detail.

Liberalism, p. 54

The meaning of economic freedom is this: that the individual is in a position to *choose* the way in which he wants to integrate himself into the totality of society.

Economic Policy, p. 17

Liberty and freedom are the conditions of man within a contractual society.

Human Action, p. 282

Freedom, as people enjoyed it in the democratic countries of Western civilization in the years of the old liberalism's triumph, was not a product of constitutions, bills of rights, laws, and statutes. Those documents aimed only at safeguarding liberty and freedom, firmly established by the operation of the market economy, against encroachments on the part of office holders. No government and no civil law can guarantee and bring about freedom otherwise than by supporting and defending the fundamental institutions of the market economy. . . . Where there is no market economy, the best-intentioned provisions of constitutions and laws remain a dead letter.

Human Action, p. 283; p. 285

The freedom of man under capitalism is an effect of competition.

Human Action, p. 283; p. 285

FREEDOM OF THE PRESS

A free press can exist only where there is private control on the means of production.

The Anti-Capitalistic Mentality, p. 55

FREEDOM OF THOUGHT

It was in the climate created by this capitalistic system of individualism that all the modern intellectual achievements thrived. Never before had mankind lived under conditions like those of the second part of the nineteenth century, when, in the civilized countries, the most momentous problems of philosophy, religion, and science could be freely discussed without any fear of reprisals on the part of the powers that be. It was an age of productive and salutary dissent.

The Ultimate Foundation of Economic Science, p. 123

FUTURE

Nothing suggests the belief that progress toward more satisfactory conditions is inevitable or a relapse into very unsatisfactory conditions impossible.

Human Action, pp. 856–57; p. 861

No sect and no political party has believed that it could afford to forgo advancing its cause by appealing to men's senses. Rhetorical bombast, music and song resound, banners wave, flowers and colors serve as symbols, and the leaders seek to attach their followers to their own person. Liberalism has nothing to do with all this. It has no party flower and no party color, no party song and no party idols, no symbols and no slogans. It has the substance and the arguments. These must lead it to victory.

Liberalism, p. 193

Therefore nothing is more important today than to enlighten public opinion about the basic differences between genuine Liberalism, which advocates the free market economy, and the various interventionist parties which are advocating government interference.

Economic Freedom and Interventionism, p. 244

GANDHI

Mahatma Gandhi expresses a loathing for the devices of the petty West and of devilish capitalism. But he travels by railroad or by motor car and, when ill, goes for treatment to a hospital equipped with the most refined instruments of Western surgery. It does not seem to occur to him that Western capital alone made it possible for the Hindus to enjoy these facilities.

Omnipotent Government, p. 102

GENIUS

In all nations and in all periods of history, intellectual exploits were the work of a few men and were appreciated only by a small elite. The many looked upon these feats with hatred and disdain, at best with indifference.

Austrian Economics: An Anthology, p. 58

A true genius is very rarely acknowledged as such by his contemporaries.

Bureaucracy, p. 13

Everything that is thought, done and accomplished is a performance of individuals. New ideas and innovations are always an achievement of uncommon men.

Human Action, pp. 859–60; p. 863

Genius does not allow itself to be hindered by any consideration for the comfort of its fellows—even of those closest to it.

Socialism, p. 85

It may well be that he who gives new values to mankind, or who is capable of so giving, suffers want and poverty. But there is no way to prevent this effectively. The creative spirit innovates necessarily. It must press forward. It must destroy the old and set the new in its place. It could not conceivably be relieved of this burden. If it were it would cease to be a pioneer. Progress cannot be organized. It is not difficult to ensure that the genius who has completed his work shall be crowned with laurel; that his mortal remains shall be laid in a grave of honor and monuments erected to his memory. But it is impossible to smooth the way that he must tread if he is to fulfill his destiny. Society can do nothing to aid progress. If it does not load the individual with quite unbreakable chains, if it does not surround the prison in which it encloses him with quite unsurmountable walls, it has done all that can be expected of it. Genius will soon find a way to win its own freedom.

Socialism, p. 167

To see and to act in advance, to follow new ways, is always the concern only of the few, the leaders.

Socialism, p. 188

The history of science is the record of the achievements of individuals who worked in isolation and, very often, met with indifference or even open hostility on the part of their contemporaries.

The Ultimate Foundation of Economic Science, p. 129

It is characteristic of very great persons to move forward to highest accomplishment out of an inner drive; others require an external impulse to overcome deep-rooted inertia and to develop their own selves.

Nation, State, and Economy, p. 213

What counts is not the data, but the mind that deals with them. The data that Galileo, Newton, Ricardo, Menger, and Freud made use of for their great discoveries lay at the disposal of every one of their contemporaries and of untold previous generations. Galileo was certainly not the first to observe the swinging motion of the chandelier in the cathedral at Pisa.

Epistemological Problems of Economics, p. 71

It is merely the routine of scientific procedure that can be taught and presented in textbooks. The power to accomplish feats of scientific achievement can be awakened only in one who already possesses the necessary intellectual gifts and strength of character. To be sure, without the foundations which mastery of the scientific technique and literature provides, nothing can be accomplished. However, the decisive factor remains the personality of the thinker.

Epistemological Problems of Economics, pp. 71–72

The first thing a genius needs is to breathe free air.

The Anti-Capitalistic Mentality, p. 108

Genius does not allow itself to be hindered by any consideration for the comfort of its fellows—even of those closest to it.

Socialism, pp. 85–85

GOD

Friedrich Wilhelm IV and Wilhelm II were quite convinced that God had invested them with special authority. . . . Many contemporaries believed alike and were ready to spend their last drop of blood in the service of the king sent to them by God.

Socialism, p. 56

But for an almighty supreme being there cannot be any dissatisfaction with the prevailing state of affairs. The Almighty does not act, because there is no state of affairs that he cannot render fully satisfactory without any action.

The Ultimate Foundation of Economic Science, p. 3

GOLD STANDARD

Every nation, whether rich or poor, powerful or feeble, can at any hour once again adopt the gold standard.

Omnipotent Government, p. 252

The gold standard has one tremendous virtue: the quantity of the money supply, under the gold standard, is independent of the policies of governments and political parties. This is its advantage. It is a form of protection against spendthrift governments.

Economic Policy, p. 65

The superiority of the gold standard consists in the fact that the value of gold develops independent of political actions.

On the Manipulation of Money and Credit, p. 90

The gold standard alone makes the determination of money's purchasing power independent of the ambitions and machinations of governments, of dictators, of political parties, and of pressure groups. The gold standard alone is what the nineteenth-century freedom-loving leaders (who championed representative government, civil liberties, and prosperity for all) called "sound money."

Planning for Freedom, p. 185

Governments deliberately sabotaged it, and still go on sabotaging it.

Planning for Freedom, p. 185

Under the gold standard gold is money and money is gold. It is immaterial whether or not the laws assign legal tender quality only to gold coins minted by the government. What counts is that these coins really contain a fixed weight of gold and that every quantity of bullion can be transformed into coins. Under the gold standard the dollar and the pound sterling were merely names for a definite weight of gold, within very narrow margins precisely determined by the laws.

Human Action, p. 425; pp. 428–29

Men have chosen the precious metals gold and silver for the money service on account of their mineralogical, physical, and chemical features. The use of money in a market economy is a praxeologically necessary fact. That gold—and not something else—is used as money is merely a historical fact and as such cannot be conceived by catallactics.

Human Action, p. 468; p. 471

The gold standard was the world standard of the age of capitalism, increasing welfare, liberty, and democracy, both political and economic. In the eyes of the free traders its main eminence was precisely the fact that it was an international standard as required by international trade and the transactions of the international money and capital market. It was the medium of exchange by means of which Western industrialism and Western capital had borne Western civilization into the remotest parts of the earth's surface, everywhere destroying the fetters of age-old prejudices and superstitions, sowing the seeds of new life and new well-being, freeing minds and souls, and creating riches unheard of before. It accompanied the triumphal unprecedented progress of Western liberalism ready to unite all nations into a community of free nations peacefully cooperating with one another.

Human Action, pp. 469–70; pp. 472–73

All those intent upon sabotaging the evolution toward welfare, peace, freedom, and democracy loathed the gold standard, and not only on account of its economic significance. In their eyes the gold standard was the labarum, the symbol, of all those doctrines and policies they wanted to destroy.

Human Action, p. 470; p. 473

The return to gold does not depend on the fulfillment of some material condition. It is an ideological problem. It presupposes only one thing: the abandonment of the illusion that increasing the quantity of money creates prosperity.

Economic Freedom and Interventionism, p. 86

The excellence of the gold standard is to be seen in the fact that it renders the determination of the monetary unit's purchasing power independent of the policies of governments and political parties.

The Theory of Money and Credit, p. 456

The gold standard did not collapse. Governments abolished it in order to pave the way for inflation. The whole grim apparatus of oppression and coercion—policemen, customs guards, penal courts, prisons, in some countries even executioners—had to be put into action in order to destroy the gold standard. Solemn pledges were broken, retroactive laws were promulgated, provisions of constitutions and bills of rights were openly defied. And hosts of servile writers praised what the governments had done and hailed the dawn of the fiat-money millennium.

The Theory of Money and Credit, p. 461

The classical or orthodox gold standard alone is a truly effective check on the power of the government to inflate the currency. Without such a check all other constitutional safeguards can be rendered vain.

The Theory of Money and Credit, p. 495

If we had gold coins in actual daily circulation everywhere in the world . . . the depreciation of gold would . . . not have taken place at all.

Money, Method, and the Market Process, p. 84

GOOD GOVERNMENT

All that good government can do to improve the material well-being of the masses is to establish and to preserve an institutional setting in which there are no obstacles to the progressive accumulation of new capital and its utilization for the improvement of technical methods of production.

Planning for Freedom, p. 6

Government ought to protect the individuals within the country against the violent and fraudulent attacks of gangsters, and it should defend the country against foreign enemies.

Economic Policy, p. 37

I do not hate the government by declaring that it is fit to do certain things but not fit to do other things.

Economic Policy, p. 38

Governments become liberal only when forced to by the citizens.

Omnipotent Government, p. 58

Whoever wants lastingly to establish good government must start by trying to persuade his fellow citizens and offering them sound ideologies. . . . There is no hope left for a civilization when the masses favor harmful policies.

Omnipotent Government, p. 120

GOOD WILL

The role which good will plays on the market does not impair or restrict competition. Everybody is free to acquire good will, and every bearer of good will can lose good will once acquired.

Human Action, p. 377; p. 380

GOVERNMENT

Government is essentially the negation of liberty.

Liberty and Property, p. 19

It is the opposite of liberty. It is beating, imprisoning, hanging.

Liberty and Property, p. 19

Government means always coercion and compulsion and is by necessity the opposite of liberty.

Human Action, p. 283; p. 285

History provides an abundance of striking examples to show that, in the long run, even the most ruthless policy of repression does not suffice to maintain a government in power.

Liberalism, p. 45

It is an illusion to expect that despotism will always side with the good causes.

Theory and History, p. 372

It is in the nature of the men handling the apparatus of compulsion and coercion to overrate its power to work, and to strive at subduing all spheres of human life to its immediate influence.

Omnipotent Government, p. 58

The government pretends to be endowed with the mystical power to accord favors out of an inexhaustible horn of plenty. It is both omniscient and omnipotent. It can by a magic wand create happiness and abundance. The truth is the government cannot give if it does not take from somebody.

Bureaucracy, p. 84

The government and its chiefs do not have the powers of the mythical Santa Claus. They cannot spend except by taking out of the pockets of some people for the benefit of others.

Planning for Freedom, p. 187

Whoever wants to see the world governed according to his own ideas must strive for dominion over men's minds. It is impossible, in the long run, to subject men against their will to a regime that they reject. Whoever tries to do so by force will ultimately come to grief, and the struggles provoked by his attempt will do more harm than the worst government based on the consent of the governed could ever do. Men cannot be made happy against their will.

Liberalism, p. 46

A liberal government is a *contradictio in adjecto*. Governments must be forced into adopting liberalism by the power of the unanimous opinion of the people; that they could voluntarily become liberal is not to be expected.

Liberalism, p. 68

Politically there is nothing more advantageous for a government than an attack on property rights, for it is always an easy matter to incite the masses against the owners of land and capital. From time immemorial, therefore, it has been the idea of all absolute monarchs, of all despots and tyrants, to ally themselves with the "people" against the propertied classes.

Liberalism, p. 69

In spite of all persecutions, however, the institution of private property has survived. Neither the animosity of all governments, nor the hostile campaign waged against it by writers and moralists and by churches and religions, nor the resentment of the masses—itself deeply rooted in instinctive envy—has availed to abolish it.

Liberalism, p. 69

Daily experience proves clearly to everybody but the most bigoted fanatics of socialism that governmental management is inefficient and wasteful.

Economic Freedom and Interventionism, p. 62

There is no remedy for the inefficiency of public management.

Economic Freedom and Interventionism, p. 63

The main problem is how to prevent the police power from becoming tyrannical. This is the meaning of all the struggles for liberty.

The Ultimate Foundation of Economic Science, p. 98

Government is a guarantor of liberty and is compatible with liberty only if its range is adequately restricted to the preservation of what is called economic freedom.

Human Action, p. 283

Once the principle is admitted that it is duty of government to protect the individual against his own foolishness, no serious objections can be advanced against further encroachments.

Human Action, pp. 728–29, p. 733

GROSS NATIONAL PRODUCT

The macroeconomic concept of national income is a mere political slogan devoid of any cognitive value.

The Ultimate Foundation of Economic Science, p. 87

GROUPS

Every collectivist assumes a different source for the collective will, according to his own political, religious and national convictions.

Socialism, p. 56

Man is not the member of one group only and does not appear on the scene of human affairs solely in the role of a member of one definitive group. In speaking of social groups it must be remembered that the members of one group are at the same time members of other groups. The conflict of groups is not a conflict between neatly integrated herds of men. It is a conflict between various concerns in the minds of individuals.

Theory and History, p. 257

GUNS

Every act of the government which can and must be done by administrative discretion with regard to the special merits of each case can be used for the achievement of the government's political aims. The members of the linguistic minority are treated like foes or like outlaws. . . . Protection is denied to their property, persons, and lives when they are attacked by armed gangs of zealous members of the ruling linguistic group. They cannot even undertake to defend themselves: the licenses required for the possession of arms are denied to them.

Omnipotent Government, p. 83

HAPPINESS

Men cannot be made happy against their will.

Liberalism, p. 46

Nobody is in a position to decree what should make a fellow man happier.

Human Action, p. 14; p. 14

Each individual is the only and final arbiter in matters concerning his own satisfaction and happiness.

Theory and History, p. 13

Nobody is called upon to determine what could make another man happier or less unhappy.

Planning for Freedom, p. 118

You do not increase the happiness of a man eager to attend a performance of *Abie's Irish Rose* by forcing him to attend a perfect performance of *Hamlet* instead. You may deride his poor taste. But he alone is supreme in matters of his own satisfaction.

Bureaucracy, pp. 90–91

There is no means of comparing and measuring the happiness of different people and of the same people at different times.

Human Action, p. 617; p. 621

If a man drinks wine and not water I cannot say he is acting irrationally. At most I can say that in his place I would not do so. But his pursuit of happiness is his own business, not mine.

Socialism, p. 405

Man is not evil merely because he wants to enjoy pleasure and avoid pain—in other words, to live. Renunciation, abnegation, and self-sacrifice are not good in themselves.

Socialism, p. 409

HEALTH

There is no clearly defined frontier between health and illness. Being ill is not a phenomenon independent of conscious will and of psychic forces working in the subconscious. A man's efficiency is not merely the result of his physical condition; it depends largely on his mind and will.

Socialism, p. 431

HISTORICAL SCHOOL

The political significance of the work of the Historical school consisted in the fact that it rendered Germany safe for the ideas, the acceptance of which made popular with the German people all those disastrous policies that resulted in the great catastrophes. The aggressive imperialism that twice ended in war and defeat, the limitless inflation of the early 1920s, the command economy and all the horrors of the Nazi regime were achievements of politicians who acted as they had been taught by the champions of the Historical school.

Austrian Economics: An Anthology, p. 67

HISTORICISM

As for the German historians, I found fault in their crude and materialistic position on power. To them power meant bayonets and cannons, and realistic policies were those relying solely on militarism. Everything else they called illusion, idealism, and utopianism.

Notes and Recollections, p. 5

HISTORY

History speaks only to those people who know how to interpret it.

Human Action, p. 859; p. 863

Historical knowledge is indispensable for those who want to build a better world.

Omnipotent Government, p. 14

History in the broadest sense of the term is the totality of human experience.

The Ultimate Foundation of Economic Science, p. 45

History should teach us to recognize causes and to understand driving forces; and when we understand everything, we will forgive everything.

Nation, State, and Economy, p. 2

It is a fact that hardly any historian has fully avoided passing judgments of value. But such judgments are always merely incidental to the genuine tasks of history. In uttering them the author speaks as an individual judging from the point of view of his personal valuations, not as a historian.

Theory and History, p. 21

The way in which the history of the last two hundred years has been treated is really a scandal.

Planning for Freedom, p. 170

There is no such thing as a nonhistorical analysis of the present state of affairs.

Theory and History, p. 287

The mere fact that an event happened in a distant country and a remote age does not in itself prove that it has no bearing on the present.

Theory and History, p. 290

Again and again, the early historians of capitalism have— one can hardly use a milder word—falsified history.

Economic Policy, p. 7

History can tell us what happened in the past. But it cannot assert that it must happen again in the future.

Human Action, p. 546; p. 549

A historian's achievement consists in presenting the past in a new perspective of understanding.

Theory and History, p. 290

History looks backward into the past, but the lesson it teaches concerns things to come. It does not teach indolent quietism; it rouses man to emulate the deeds of earlier generations.

Theory and History, p. 294

Neither as judges allotting praise and blame nor as avengers seeking out the guilty should we face the past. We seek truth, not guilt; we want to know how things came about to understand them, not to issue condemnations.

Nation, State, and Economy, p. 1

It is not the task of history to gratify the need of the masses for heroes and scapegoats.

Nation, State, and Economy, p. 1

It is not the task of history to project the hatred and disagreements of the present back into the past and to draw from battles fought long ago weapons for the disputes of one's own time.

Nation, State, and Economy, p. 2

History makes one wise, but not competent to solve concrete problems.

Epistemological Problems of Economics, p. xxiii

If history could teach us anything, it would be that private property is inextricably linked with civilization.

Omnipotent Government, p. 58

Every action adds something to history, affects the course of future events, and is in this sense a historical fact. The most trivial performance of daily routine by dull people is no less a historical datum than is the most startling innovation of the genius.

Theory and History, p. 195

HUMAN FRAILTY

As human nature is, everybody is prone to overrate his own worth and deserts.

The Anti-Capitalistic Mentality, p. 13

If one rejects laissez faire on account of man's fallibility and moral weakness, one must for the same reasons also reject every kind of government action.

Planning for Freedom, p. 44

IDEAS

Only ideas can overcome ideas.

Socialism, p. 460

We must fight all that we dislike in public life. We must substitute better ideas for wrong ideas. We must refute the doctrines that promote union violence.

Economic Policy, p. 105

Everything that happens in the social world in our time is the result of ideas. Good things and bad things. What is needed is to fight bad ideas. We must oppose the confiscation of property, the control of prices, inflation, and all those evils from which we suffer.

Economic Policy, p. 105

Both force and money are impotent against ideas.

Omnipotent Government, p. 210

The ideas that change the intellectual climate of a given environment are those unheard of before. For these new ideas there is no other explanation than that there was a man from whose mind they originated.

The Ultimate Foundation of Economic Science, p. 91

One cannot "organize" or "institutionalize" the emergence of new ideas.

The Ultimate Foundation of Economic Science, p. 129

In a battle between force and an idea, the latter always prevails.

Liberalism, p. 50

Great conflicts of ideas must be solved by straight and frank methods; they cannot be solved by artifices and makeshifts.

Planning for Freedom, p. 14

Thoughts and ideas are not phantoms. They are real things. Although intangible and immaterial, they are factors in bringing about changes in the realm of tangible and material things.

Theory and History, p. 96

No mass phenomenon can be adequately treated without analyzing the ideas implied. And no new ideas spring from the mythical mind of the masses.

Theory and History, p. 263

In the long run even the most despotic governments with all their brutality and cruelty are no match for ideas. Eventually the ideology that has won the support of the majority will prevail and cut the ground from under the tyrant's feet. Then the oppressed many will rise in rebellion and overthrow their masters.

Theory and History, p. 372

Ideas live longer than walls and other material artifacts.

Theory and History, p. 196

No one can find a safe way out for himself if society is sweeping towards destruction. Therefore everyone, in his own interests, must thrust himself vigorously into the intellectual battle. None can stand aside with unconcern; the interests of everyone hang on the result. Whether he chooses or not, every man is drawn into the great historical struggle, the decisive battle into which our epoch has plunged us.

Socialism, pp. 468–69

IDEOLOGY

No one can escape the influence of a prevailing ideology.

Epistemological Problems of Economics, p. 197

There is no use in dealing in a summary way with any ideology however foolish and contradictory it may appear. Even a manifestly erroneous doctrine should be refuted by careful analysis and the unmasking of the fallacies implied. A sound doctrine can win only by exploding the delusions of its adversaries.

The Theory of Money and Credit, pp. 455–56

IMMIGRATION

There cannot be the slightest doubt that migration barriers diminish the productivity of human labor.

Liberalism, p. 139

The closed-door policy is one of the root causes of our wars.

Omnipotent Government, p. 263

Immigrants soon find their place in urban life, they soon adopt, externally, town manners and opinions, but for a long time they remain foreign to civic thought. One cannot make a social philosophy one's own as easily as a new costume. . . . More menacing than barbarians storming the walls from without are the seeming citizens within—those who are citizens in gesture, but not in thought.

Socialism, p. 38

IMPERIALISM

Neither fame nor honor nor wealth nor happiness was to be found on this path.

Nation, State, and Economy, p. 75

The welfare of a people lies not in casting other peoples down but in peaceful collaboration.

Nation, State, and Economy, p. 75

The imperialistic people's state scarcely differs from the old principle state in its interpretation of sovereignty and its boundaries. Like the latter, it knows no other limits to the expansion of its rule than those drawn by the opposition of an equally strong power. Even its lust for conquest is unlimited. It wants to hear nothing of the right of peoples. If it "needs" a territory, then it simply takes it and, where possible, demands further from the subjugated peoples that they find this just and reasonable. Foreign peoples are in its eyes not subjects but objects of policy.

Nation, State, and Economy, p. 79

Nothing is more stupid than efforts to justify today's imperialism, with all of its brutalities, by reference to atrocities of generations long since gone.

Nation, State, and Economy, p. 76

For fully developed imperialism, the individual no longer has value. He is valuable to it only as a member of the whole, as a soldier of an army.

Nation, State, and Economy, p. 78

Marxian socialism, as a fundamentally revolutionary movement, is inwardly inclined toward imperialism. No one will dispute that, least of all the Marxists themselves, who straightforwardly proclaim the cult of revolution. It is less noted, however, that modern socialism of necessity must be imperialistic outwardly also.

Nation, State, and Economy, p. 206

Modern imperialism is distinguished from the expansionist tendencies of the absolute principalities by the fact that its moving spirits are not the members of the ruling dynasty, nor even of the nobility, the Bureaucracy, or the officers' corps of the army bent on personal enrichment and aggrandizement by plundering the resources of conquered territories, but the mass of the people, who look upon it as the most appropriate means for the preservation of national independence.

Liberalism, p. 122

INDEX CALCULATION

Even if the fundamental difficulties standing in the way of index calculations could be overcome, the practical difficulties remaining would still be very great.

Money, Method, and the Market Process, p. 88

INDIVIDUALISM

On the market it is not mankind, the state, or the corporative unit that acts, but individual men and groups of men, and that *their* valuations and *their* actions are decisive, not those of abstract collectives. . . . This discovery signaled nothing less than a Copernican revolution in social science.

Austrian Economics: An Anthology, p. 125

In the history of the last two hundred years we can discern . . . the trend toward freedom, the rights of man, and self-determination. This individualism resulted in the fall of autocratic government, the establishment of democracy, the evolution of capitalism, technical improvements, and an unprecedented rise in standards of living. It substituted enlightenment for old superstitions, scientific methods of research for inveterate prejudices. It was an epoch of great artistic and literary achievements, the age of immortal musicians, painters, writers, and philosophers. And it brushed away slavery, serfdom, torture, inquisition, and other remnants of the dark ages.

Omnipotent Government, p. 8

The philosophy that is the characteristic mark of the West and whose consistent elaboration has in the last centuries transformed all social institutions has been called individualism. It maintains that ideas, the good ones as well as the bad, originate in the mind of an individual man.

Theory and History, p. 371

INDUSTRIAL REVOLUTION

The factory owners did not have the power to compel anybody to take a factory job. They could only hire people who were ready to work for the wages offered to them. Low as these wage rates were, they were nonetheless much more than these paupers could earn in any other field open to them. It is a distortion of facts to say that the factories carried off the housewives from the nurseries and the kitchens and the children from their play. These women had nothing to cook with and to feed their children. These children were destitute and starving. Their only refuge was the factory. It saved them, in the strict sense of the term, from death by starvation.

Human Action, p. 615; pp. 619–20

The outstanding fact about the Industrial Revolution is that it opened an age of mass production for the needs of the masses. The wage earners are no longer people toiling merely for other people's well-being. They themselves are the main consumers of the products the factories turn out. Big business depends upon mass consumption.

Human Action, p. 616; p. 621

The market economy itself was not a product of violent action—of revolutions—but of a series of gradual peaceful changes. The implications of the term "industrial revolution" are utterly misleading.

The Ultimate Foundation of Economic Science, p. 109

The mothers who worked in the factories had nothing to cook with; they did not leave their homes and their kitchens to go into the factories, they went into factories because they had no kitchens, and if they had a kitchen they had no food to cook in those kitchens. And the children did not come from comfortable nurseries. They were starving and dying.

Economic Policy, pp. 6–7

INFANT INDUSTRIES

The infant industries argument advanced in favor of protective tariffs represents a hopeless attempt to justify such measures on a purely economic basis, without regard to political considerations. It is a grievous error to fail to recognize the political motivation behind the demand for tariffs on behalf of infant industries.

Epistemological Problems of Economics, p. 223

INFLATION

Continued inflation inevitably leads to catastrophe.

Defense, Controls, and Inflation, p. 109

The assistance of inflation is invoked whenever a government is unwilling to increase taxation or unable to raise a loan; that is the truth of the matter.

The Theory of Money and Credit, p. 253

What people today call inflation is not inflation, i.e., the increase in the quantity of money and money substitutes, but the general rise in commodity prices and wage rates which is the inevitable consequence of inflation. This semantic innovation is by no means harmless.

Planning for Freedom, p. 79

But the certain fact about inflation is that, sooner or later, it must come to an end. It is a policy that cannot last.

Economic Policy, p. 63

The most important thing to remember is that inflation is not an act of God, that inflation is not a catastrophe of the elements or a disease that comes like the plague. Inflation is a *policy*.

Economic Policy, p. 72

Money, like chocolate on a hot oven, was melting in the pockets of the people.

Economic Policy, p. 65

Inflation can be pursued only so long as the public still does not believe it will continue. Once the people generally realize that the inflation will be continued on and on and that the value of the monetary unit will decline more and more, then the fate of the money is sealed. Only the belief, that the inflation will come to a stop, maintains the value of the notes.

On the Manipulation of Money and Credit, p. 16

Inflationism, however, is not an isolated phenomenon. It is only one piece in the total framework of politico-economic and socio-philosophical ideas of our time. Just as the sound money policy of gold standard advocates went hand in hand with liberalism, free trade, capitalism and peace, so is inflationism part and parcel of imperialism, militarism, protectionism, statism and socialism.

On the Manipulation of Money and Credit, p. 48

Inflation and credit expansion, the preferred methods of present day government openhandedness, do not add anything to the amount of resources available. They make some people more prosperous, but only to the extent that they make others poorer.

Bureaucracy, p. 84

The pretended solicitude for the nation's welfare, for the public in general, and for the poor ignorant masses in particular was a mere blind. The governments wanted inflation and credit expansion, they wanted booms and easy money.

Human Action, p. 438; p. 441

It would be a serious blunder to neglect the fact that inflation also generates forces which tend toward capital consumption. One of its consequences is that it falsifies economic calculation and accounting. It produces the phenomenon of illusory or apparent profits.

Human Action, p. 546; p. 549

If inflation is pushed to its ultimate consequences, it makes any stipulation of deferred payments in terms of the inflated currency cease altogether.

Human Action, p. 779; p. 785

Credit expansion and inflationary increase of the quantity of money frustrate the "common man's" attempts to save and to accumulate reserves for less propitious days.

Human Action, p. 834; p. 838

Inflation is essentially antidemocratic.

Omnipotent Government, p. 252

The advocates of public control cannot do without inflation. They need it in order to finance their policy of reckless spending and of lavishly subsidizing and bribing the voters.

The Theory of Money and Credit, p. 479

One can say without exaggeration that inflation is an indispensable intellectual means of militarism. Without it, the repercussions of war on welfare would become obvious much more quickly and penetratingly; war-weariness would set in much earlier.

Nation, State, and Economy, p. 163

No complaint is more widespread than that against "dearness of living." There has been no generation that has not grumbled about the "expensive times" that it lives in. But the fact that "everything" is becoming dearer simply means that the objective exchange value of money is falling.

The Theory of Money and Credit, p. 177

Who has any doubt that the belligerent peoples of Europe would have tired of war much more quickly if their governments had clearly and candidly laid before them at the time the account of their war expenditure?

The Theory of Money and Credit, p. 254

Inflation has always been an important resource of policies of war and revolution and why we also find it in the service of socialism.

The Theory of Money and Credit, p. 255

Inflation is the fiscal complement of statism and arbitrary government. It is a cog in the complex of policies and institutions which gradually lead toward totalitarianism.

The Theory of Money and Credit, p. 468

No emergency can justify a return to inflation. Inflation can provide neither the weapons a nation needs to defend its independence nor the capital goods required for any project. It does not cure unsatisfactory conditions. It merely helps the rulers whose policies brought about the catastrophe to exculpate themselves.

The Theory of Money and Credit, p. 481

Inflation is the true opium of the people and it is administered to them by anticapitalist governments and parties.

The Theory of Money and Credit, p. 485

INSTINCT

Every doctrine denying to the "single paltry individual" any role in history must finally ascribe changes and improvements to the operation of instincts. As those upholding such doctrines see it, man is an animal that has the instinct to produce poems, cathedrals, and airplanes. Civilization is the result of an unconscious and unpremeditated reaction of man to external stimuli. Each achievement is the automatic creation of an instinct with which man has been endowed especially for this purpose. There are as many instincts as there are human achievements. It is needless to enter into a critical examination of this fable invented by impotent people for slighting the achievements of better men and appealing to the resentment of the dull. Even on the basis of this makeshift doctrine one cannot negate the distinction between the man who had the instinct to write the book *On the Origin of Species* and those who lacked this instinct.

Theory and History, p. 194–95

INTELLECTUALS

They coined most of the slogans that guided the butcheries of Bolshevism, Fascism, and Nazism. Intellectuals extolling the delights of murder, writers advocating censorship, philosophers judging the merits of thinkers and authors, not according to the value of their contributions but according to their achievements on battlefields, are the spiritual leaders of our age of perpetual strife.

Austrian Economics: An Anthology, p. 75

Only the literati are enthusiastic about poverty, i.e., the poverty of others. The rest of mankind, however, prefer prosperity to misery.

Epistemological Problems of Economics, p. 92

The intellectual leaders of the peoples have produced and propagated the fallacies which are on the point of destroying liberty and Western civilization.

Planned Chaos, p. 90

It is certain that many intellectuals envy the higher income of prosperous businessmen and that these feelings drive them toward socialism. They believe that the authorities of a socialist commonwealth would pay them higher salaries than those that they earn under capitalism.

Human Action, p. 90; p. 90

American authors or scientists are prone to consider the wealthy businessman as a barbarian, as a man exclusively intent upon making money.

The Anti-Capitalistic Mentality, p. 20

There are people to whom monetary calculation is repulsive. They do not want to be roused from their daydreams by the voice of critical reason. Reality sickens them, they long for a realm of unlimited opportunity. They are disgusted by the meanness of a social order in which everything is nicely reckoned in dollars and pennies.

Human Action, p. 231; p. 230

Many "progressive" professors have for some time served in one of the various alphabetical government agencies. . . . They compiled statistics and wrote memoranda which their superiors, either politicians or former managers of corporations, filed without reading. The professors did not instill a scientific spirit into the bureaus. But the bureaus gave them the mentality of authoritarianism. They distrust the populace and consider the State (with a capital S) as the God-sent guardian of the wretched underlings. Only the Government is impartial and unbiased. Whoever opposes any expansion of governmental powers is by this token unmasked as an enemy of the commonweal.

Planning for Freedom, p. 167

The first socialists were the intellectuals; they and not the masses are the backbone of Socialism.

Socialism, p. 461

Almost all the fathers of socialism were members of the upper middle class or of the professions.

Omnipotent Government, p. 118

From the political point of view it is no doubt dangerous that men are so easily stirred by bombastic talk. But the political actions of modern nationalism cannot be explained or excused by chauvinist intoxication. They are the outcome of cool though misguided reasoning. The carefully elaborated, although erroneous, doctrines of scholarly and thoughtful books have led to the clash of nations, to bloody wars, and destruction.

Omnipotent Government, p. 125

The educated classes are possessed by the idea that in the social domain anything can be accomplished if only one applies enough force and is sufficiently resolute.

Epistemological Problems of Economics, p. 200

Every new theory encounters opposition and rejection at first. The adherents of the old, accepted doctrine object to the new theory, refuse it recognition, and declare it to be mistaken. Years, even decades, must pass before it succeeds in supplanting the old one. A new generation must grow up before its victory is decisive.

Epistemological Problems of Economics, p. 184

INTEREST RATE

Interest is the difference in the valuation of present goods and future goods; it is the discount in the valuation of future goods as against that of present goods.

Planning for Freedom, pp. 187–88

The height of the market rate of interest ultimately does not depend on the whims, fancies, and the pecuniary interests of the personnel operating the government apparatus of coercion and compulsion, the much-referred-to "public sector" of the economy.

Planning for Freedom, p. 188

It cannot be denied that everyone is inclined—especially among the borrowers of this lowest category—to overestimate his own credit rating, and call the rates demanded by creditors too high.

A Critique of Interventionism, p. 49

Public opinion always wants "easy money," that is, low interest rates.

A Critique of Interventionism, p. 163

There cannot be any question of abolishing interest by any institutions, laws, or devices of bank manipulation. He who wants to "abolish" interest will have to induce people to value an apple available in a hundred years no less than a present apple. What can be abolished by laws and decrees is merely the right of the capitalist to receive interest. But such decrees would bring about capital consumption and would very soon throw mankind back into the original state of natural poverty.

Human Action, p. 529; p. 532

The expectation of rising prices thus has the tendency to make the gross rate of interest rise, while the expectation of dropping prices makes it drop.

Human Action, p. 540; p. 543

The greater the fund of means of subsistence in a community, the lower the rate of interest.

The Theory of Money and Credit, p. 386

INTERNATIONAL LAW

All attempts to create a substantive international law through whose application disputes among nations could be decided have miscarried.

Nation, State, and Economy, p. 90

[Y]ou simply cannot argue with nationalists. The Germans are fully convinced that compulsion applied by them to other nations is fair and just, while compulsion applied to themselves is criminal.

Omnipotent Government, pp. 257–58

No international authority can preserve peace if economic wars continue. In our age of international division of labor, free trade is the prerequisite for any amicable arrangement between nations. And free trade is impossible in a world of etatism.

Omnipotent Government, p. 6

INTERNATIONAL MONETARY COOPERATION

What governments call international monetary cooperation is concerted action for the sake of credit expansion.

Human Action, p. 473; p. 476

INTERNATIONAL MONETARY FUND

Even the manifest futility of the International Monetary Fund does not deter authors from indulging in dreams about a world bank fertilizing mankind with floods of cheap credit.

The Theory of Money and Credit, pp. 477–78

INTERNATIONAL TRADE

The world community of labor is based on the reciprocal advantage of all participants. Whoever wants to maintain and extend it must renounce all resentment in advance.

Nation, State, and Economy, p. 220

Foreign trade differs from domestic trade only in so far as goods and services are exchanged beyond the borderlines separating the territories of two sovereign nations.

Human Action, p. 662; p. 666

It is a matter of indifference whether one produces food-stuffs and raw materials at home oneself or, if it seems more economic, obtains them from abroad in exchange for other products that one has produced.

Nation, State, and Economy, p. 84

Imports are in fact paid for by exports and not by money.

The Theory of Money and Credit, p. 286

INTERVENTIONISM

The essence of the interventionist policy is to take from one group to give to another. It is confiscation and distribution.

Human Action, p. 851; p. 855

If all interventionist laws were really to be observed they would soon lead to absurdity.

A Critique of Interventionism, p. 30

Socialism and interventionism. Both have in common the goal of subordinating the individual unconditionally to the state.

Omnipotent Government, p. 44

Economic interventionism is a self-defeating policy. The individual measures that it applies do not achieve the results sought. They bring about a state of affairs, which—from the viewpoint of its advocates themselves—is much more undesirable than the previous state they intended to alter.

Bureaucracy, p. 119

Interventionism cannot be considered as an economic system destined to stay. It is a method for the transformation of capitalism into socialism by a series of successive steps.

Planning for Freedom, p. 28

The middle-of-the-road policy is not an economic system that can last. It is a method for the realization of socialism by installments.

Planning for Freedom, pp. 32–33

The effect of its interference is that people are prevented from using their knowledge and abilities, their labor and their material means of production in the way in which they would earn the highest returns and satisfy their needs as much as possible. Such interference makes people poorer and less satisfied.

Human Action, p. 736; p. 743

On the unhampered market there prevails an irresistible tendency to employ every factor of production for the best possible satisfaction of the most urgent needs of the consumers. If the government interferes with this process, it can only impair satisfaction; it can never improve it.

Human Action, pp. 736–37; pp. 743–44

But for the inefficiency of the law-givers and the laxity, carelessness, and corruption of many of the functionaries, the last vestiges of the market economy would have long since disappeared.

Human Action, No Entry; p. 859

If the State takes the power of disposal from the owner piecemeal, by extending its influence over production; if its power to determine what direction production shall take and what kind of production there shall be, is increased, then the owner is left at last with nothing except the empty name of ownership, and property has passed into the hands of the State.

Socialism, p. 45

Every step that leads away from private ownership of the means of production and the use of money is a step away from rational economic activity.

Socialism, p. 102

State interference in economic life, which calls itself "economic policy," has done nothing but destroy economic life. Prohibitions and regulations have by their general obstructive tendency fostered the growth of the spirit of wastefulness.

Socialism, p. 424

It is indeed one of the principal drawbacks of every kind of interventionism that it is so difficult to reverse the process.

Socialism, p. 440

Every step which leads from capitalism toward planning is necessarily a step nearer to absolutism and dictatorship.

Omnipotent Government, p. 53

INVESTMENT

There is no such thing as a nonspeculative investment. In a changing economy action always involves speculation. Investments may be good or bad, but they are always speculative.

Human Action, p. 514; p. 517

JUDGMENT

All judgments of value are personal and subjective. There are no judgments of value other than those asserting *I* prefer, *I* like better, *I* wish.

Theory and History, p. 22

JUSTICE

The notion of justice makes sense only when referring to a definite system of norms which in itself is assumed to be uncontested and safe against any criticism.

Human Action, p. 716; p. 720

There is no such thing as an absolute notion of justice not referring to a definite system of social organization. . . . There is neither right nor wrong outside the social nexus.

Human Action, p. 717; p. 721

The idea of justice refers always to social cooperation.

Human Action, p. 717; p. 721

Conduct suited to preserve social cooperation is just, conduct detrimental to the preservation of society is unjust.

Theory and History, p. 54

KANT, IMMANUEL

It is nonsensical to consider Kant a precursor of Nazism. Kant advocated eternal peace between nations.

Omnipotent Government, pp. 140–41

In his book on *Eternal Peace*, the German philosopher Immanuel Kant (1724–1804) suggested that government should be forbidden to finance wars by borrowing. He expected that the warlike spirit would dwindle if all countries had to pay cash for their wars.

Economic Freedom and Interventionism, p. 99.

KEYNES

A dictum of Lord Keynes: "In the long run we are all dead." I do not question the truth of this statement; I even consider it as the only correct declaration of the neo-British Cambridge school.

Planning for Freedom, p. 7

It is the typical policy of *après nous le déluge*. Lord Keynes, the champion of this policy, says: "In the long run we are all dead." But unfortunately nearly all of us outlive the short run. We are destined to spend decades paying for the easy money orgy of a few years.

Omnipotent Government, p. 252

For what many people have admiringly called Keynes's "brilliance of style" and "mastery of language" were, in fact, cheap rhetorical tricks.

Planning for Freedom, p. 55

The unprecedented success of Keynesianism is due to the fact that it provides an apparent justification for the "deficit spending" policies of contemporary governments. It is the pseudo-philosophy of those who can think of nothing else than to dissipate the capital accumulated by previous generations.

Planning for Freedom, p. 71

Keynes did not teach us how to perform the "miracle . . . of turning a stone into bread," but the not at all miraculous procedure of eating the seed corn.

Planning for Freedom, p. 71

What he really did was to write an apology for the prevailing policies of governments.

Planning for Freedom, p. 69

The essence of Keynesianism is its complete failure to conceive the role that saving and capital accumulation play in the improvement of economic conditions.

Planning for Freedom, p. 207

They [Keynesians] blithely assume that the state has unlimited means at its disposal.

Planning for Freedom, p. 90

After 15 million human beings had perished in the war, the foremost statesmen of the world were assembled to give mankind a new international order and lasting peace . . . and the British Empire's financial expert was amused by the rustic style of the French Prime Minister's footwear.

Planning for Freedom, p. 56

In old fashioned language, Keynes proposed cheating the workers.

Economic Policy, p. 70

Keynes did not add any new idea to the body of inflationist fallacies, a thousand times refuted by economists. His teachings were even more contradictory and inconsistent than those of his predecessors who, like Silvio Gesell, were dismissed as monetary cranks. He merely knew how to cloak the plea for inflation and credit expansion in the sophisticated terminology of mathematical economics.

Human Action, p. 787; p. 793

The fallacies implied in the Keynesian full-employment doctrine are, in a new attire, essentially the same errors which [Adam] Smith and [Jean Baptiste] Say long since demolished.

The Theory of Money and Credit, p. 464

Keynes did not refute Say's Law. He rejected it emotionally, but he did not advance a single tenable argument to invalidate its rationale.

Planning for Freedom, p. 70

KNOWLEDGE

Man can never become omniscient. He can never be absolutely certain that his inquiries were not misled and that what he considers as certain truth is not error. All that man can do is to submit all his theories again and again to the most critical reexamination.

Human Action, p. 68; p. 68

Every branch of knowledge has its own merits and its own rights. Economists have never tried to belittle or deny the significance of economic history. Neither do real historians object to the study of economics.

Human Action, p. 864; p. 868

Human reasoning does not have the power to exhaust completely the content of the universe.

Epistemological Problems of Economics, p. 48

Cognition is furthered only by clarity and distinctness, never by compromises.

Epistemological Problems of Economics, p. 206

LABOR

Wages are not paid for labor expended, but for the achievements of labor, which differ widely in quality and quantity.

Human Action, p. 134; p. 134

Free labor is incomparably more productive than slave labor.

LAISSEZ FAIRE

If one rejects laissez faire on account of man's fallibility and moral weakness, one must for the same reason also reject every kind of government action.

Planning for Freedom, p. 44

Laissez faire does not mean: let soulless mechanical forces operate. It means: let individuals choose how they want to cooperate in the social division of labor and let them determine what the entrepreneurs should produce. Planning means: let the government alone choose and enforce its rulings by the apparatus of coercion and compulsion.

Planning for Freedom, p. 45

Laissez faire means: Let the common man choose and act; do not force him to yield to a dictator.

Human Action, p. 727; p. 732

Laissez faire, laissez passer does not mean: let the evils last. On the contrary, it means: do not interfere with the operation of the market because such interference must necessarily restrict output and make people poorer. It means furthermore: do not abolish or cripple the capitalist system which, in spite of all obstacles put in its way by governments and politicians, has raised the standard of living of the masses in an unprecedented way.

Omnipotent Government, p. x

What transformed the world of horse-drawn carriages, sailing ships, and windmills step by step into a world of airplanes and electronics was the laissez-faire principle.

The Ultimate Foundation of Economic Science, p. 127

The greatness of the nineteenth century consisted in the fact that to some extent the ideas of Classical economics became the dominant philosophy of state and society. They transformed the traditional status society into nations of free citizens, royal absolutism into representative government, and above all, the poverty of the masses . . . into the well-being of the many under capitalistic laissez faire.

The Historical Setting of the Austrian School, p. 44

LANGUAGE

The most important medium for social co-operation is language. Language bridges the chasm between individuals and only with its help can one man communicate to another something at least of what he is feeling . . . without it, there could be no thought but only instinct, no will but only impulse.

Socialism, p. 286

Nothing links men more closely together than a community of language, and nothing segregates them more effectively than a difference of language.

Omnipotent Government, p. 123

With the progress of the semantic confusion which has converted the meaning of political terms into their very opposite, the epithet "democratic" is now lavishly spent.

Human Action, p. 838; p. 842

Community of language binds and difference of language separates persons and peoples.

Nation, State, and Economy, p. 13

Thought is bound up with speech. The thinker's conceptual edifice is built on the elements of language.

Socialism, p. 286

Whoever wants to speak with his fellow men and to understand what they say must use their language. Everyone must therefore strive to understand and speak the language of his environment. For that reason individuals and minorities adopt the language of the majority.

Nation, State, and Economy, pp. 27–28

Once the youth learns the language of the country, however, there begins that process of adaptation to the environment that finally leads to complete assimilation.

Nation, State, and Economy, p. 117

LAW

Liberalism, which demands full freedom of the economy, seeks to dissolve the difficulties that the diversity of political arrangements pits against the development of trade by separating the economy from the state. It strives for the greatest possible unification of law, in the last analysis for world unity of law. But it does not believe that to reach this goal, great empires or even a world empire must be created.

Nation, State, and Economy, pp. 37–38

No wonder that all who have had something new to offer humanity have had nothing good to say of the state or its laws!

Liberalism, p. 58

The total complex of the rules according to which those at the helm employ compulsion and coercion is called law. Yet the characteristic feature of the state is not these rules, as such, but the application or threat of violence. A state whose chiefs recognize but one rule, to do whatever seems at the moment to be expedient in their eyes, is a state without law. It does not make any difference whether or not these tyrants are "benevolent."

Omnipotent Government, p. 46

The moral precepts and the laws of the country are means by which men seek to attain certain ends. Whether or not these ends can really be attained this way depends on the laws of the universe. The man-made laws are suitable if they are fit to attain these ends and contrary to purpose if they are not. They are open to examination from the point of view of their suitableness or unsuitableness.

Human Action, p. 756; pp. 761–62

What counts is not the letter of the law but the substantive content of the legal norm.

Nation, State, and Economy, p. 173

LAW OF THE JUNGLE

What elevates man above all other animals is the cognition that peaceful cooperation under the principle of the division of labor is a better method to preserve life and to remove felt uneasiness than indulging in pitiless biological competition for a share in the scarce means of subsistence provided by nature. Guided by this insight, man alone among all living beings consciously aims at substituting social cooperation for what philosophers have called the state of nature or *bellum omnium contra omnes* or the law of the jungle.

The Ultimate Foundation of Economic Science, p. 97

LEISURE

Among the amenities which civilized man can enjoy in a more abundant way than his less civilized ancestors there is also the enjoyment of more leisure time.

Human Action, p. 133; p. 133

LENIN

Lenin's ideal was to build a nation's production effort according to the model of the post office.

Liberty and Property, p. 14

In his life and his reading he remained so far removed from the facts of economic life that he was as great a stranger to the work of the bourgeoisie as a Hottentot to the work of an explorer taking geographical measurements.

Socialism, p. 189

Lenin was cynical enough to say that revolutions must be achieved with the catchwords of the day. And he achieved his own revolution by affirming publicly—against his better conviction—the catchwords that had taken hold of public opinion.

Omnipotent Government, p. 127

All that Lenin learned about business from the tales of his comrades who occasionally sat in business offices was that it required a lot of scribbling, recording, and ciphering. Thus, he declares that "accounting and control" are the chief things necessary for the organizing and correct functioning of society. . . . Here we have the philosophy of the filing clerk in its full glory.

The Anti-Capitalistic Mentality, pp. 24–25

LIBERTY

Liberty is always freedom from the government.

Liberty and Property, p. 19

It is a fact that a hundred years ago only a few people anticipated the over-powering momentum which the anti-libertarian ideas were destined to acquire in a very short time. The ideal of liberty seemed to be so firmly rooted that everybody thought that no reactionary movement could ever succeed in eradicating it.

The Anti-Capitalistic Mentality, p. 94

LITERATURE

Literature is not conformism, but dissent. Those authors who merely repeat what everybody approves and wants to hear are of no importance. What counts alone is the innovator, the dissenter, the harbinger of things unheard of, the man who rejects the traditional standards and aims at substituting new values and ideas for old ones. He is by necessity anti-authoritarian and anti-governmental, irreconcilably opposed to the immense majority of his contemporaries. He is precisely the author whose books the greater part of the public does not buy.

The Anti-Capitalistic Mentality, p. 51

It is true that most of the novels and plays published today are mere trash. Nothing else can be expected when thousands of volumes are written every year. Our age could still some day be called an age of the flowering of literature if only one out of a thousand books published would prove to be equal to the great books of the past.

The Anti-Capitalistic Mentality, p. 52

It is not the fault of capitalism that the common man does not appreciate uncommon books.

The Anti-Capitalistic Mentality, p. 52

What characterizes capitalism is not the bad taste of the crowds, but the fact that these crowds, made prosperous by capitalism, became "consumers" of literature—of course, of trashy literature. The book market is flooded by a downpour of trivial faction for the semibarbarians. But this does not prevent great authors from creating imperishable works.

The Anti-Capitalistic Mentality, p. 79

LOGIC

The logical structure of human thought is immutable throughout the whole course of time and is the same for all races, nations, and classes.

Epistemological Problems of Economics, p. 204

We can speak to each other only because we can appeal to something common to all of us, namely, the logical structure of reason.

Omnipotent Government, p. 143

Polylogism denies the uniformity of the logical structure of the human mind. Every social class, every nation, race, or period of history is equipped with a logic that differs from the logic of other classes, nations, races, or ages. Hence bourgeois economics differs from proletarian economics, German physics from the physics of other nations, Aryan mathematics from Semitic mathematics.

Theory and History, pp. 31–32

Polylogism is not a philosophy or an epistemological theory. It is an attitude of narrow-minded fanatics, who cannot imagine that anybody could be more reasonable or more clever than they themselves. Nor is polylogism scientific. It is rather the replacement of reasoning and science by superstitions. It is the characteristic mentality of an age of chaos.

Omnipotent Government, p. 147

LOOPHOLE

What is a loophole? If the law does not punish a definite action or does not tax a definite thing, this is not a loophole. It is simply the law.

Defense, Controls, and Inflation, p. 115

LOVE

The evolution which has led from the principle of violence to the contractual principle has based these relations on free choice in love. The woman may deny herself to anyone, she may demand fidelity and constancy from the man to whom she gives herself. Only in this way is the foundation laid for the development of woman's individuality.

Socialism, p. 91

The truth is that love and marriage were separate and people did not expect marriage to give them lasting and unclouded happiness. Only when the idea of contract and consent has been imposed on marriage does the wedded couple demand that their union shall satisfy desire permanently.

Socialism, p. 85

LUXURIES

Luxury is the roadmaker of progress.

Socialism, p. 177

Every innovation makes its appearance as a "luxury" of the few well-to-do. After industry has become aware of it, the luxury then becomes a "necessity" for all.

A Critique of Interventionism, p. 158

The luxury of today is the necessity of tomorrow. Every advance first comes into being as the luxury of a few rich people, only to become, after a time, an indispensable necessity taken for granted by everyone. Luxury consumption provides industry with the stimulus to discover and introduce new, things. It is one of the dynamic factors in our economy. To it we owe the progressive innovations by which the standard of living of all strata of the population has been gradually raised.

Liberalism, p. 32

In so far as they think consistently, moralists who condemn luxury must recommend the comparatively desireless existence of the wild life roaming in the woods as the ultimate ideal of civilized life.

Socialism, p. 177

Most of us have no sympathy with the rich idler who spends his life in pleasure without ever doing any work. But even he fulfills a function in the life of the social organism. He sets an example of luxury that awakens in the multitude a consciousness of new needs and gives industry the incentive to fulfill them.

Liberalism, pp. 32–33

A great deal of what people in less capitalistic countries consider luxury is a common good in the more capitalistically developed countries.

A Critique of Interventionism, p. 158

MAJORITY RULE

In the political field it is always the will of the majority that prevails, and the minorities must yield to it.

Liberty and Property, p. 12

In the political sphere, there is no means for an individual or a small group of individuals to disobey the will of the majority. But in the intellectual field private property makes rebellion possible.

Liberty and Property, p. 12

[They knew that] all men are liable to error and that it could happen that the majority, deluded by faulty doctrines propagated by irresponsible demagogues, could embark upon policies that would result in disaster, even in the entire destruction of civilization.

The Ultimate Foundation of Economic Science, p. 93

When any sort of difference arises between law and opinion, a reaction must necessarily follow; a movement sets in against that part of the law that is felt to be unjust. Such conflicts always tend to end in a victory of opinion over the law; ultimately the views of the ruling class become embodied in the law.

The Theory of Money and Credit, p. 229

MARKET

Within the market society each serves all his fellow citizens and each is served by them. It is a system of mutual exchange of services and commodities, a mutual giving and receiving.

Omnipotent Government, p. 49

The fundamental law of the market is: the customer is always right.

Economic Freedom and Interventionism, p. 6

MARKET PROCESS

The market process is a daily repeated plebiscite, and it ejects inevitably from the ranks of profitable people those who do not employ their property according to the orders given by the public.

Liberty and Property, p. 10

MARRIAGE

As the idea of contract enters the Law of Marriage, it breaks the rule of the male, and makes the wife a partner with equal rights. From a one-sided relationship resting on force, marriage thus becomes a mutual agreement.

Socialism, p. 82

Thus marriage, as we know it, has come into existence entirely as a result of the contractual idea penetrating into this sphere of life. All our cherished ideals of marriage have grown out of this idea. That marriage unites one man and one woman, that it can be entered into only with the free will of both parties, that it imposes a duty of mutual fidelity, that a man's violations of the marriage vows are to be judged no differently from a woman's, that the rights of husband and wife are essentially the same—these principles develop from the contractual attitude to the problem of marital life.

Socialism, pp. 82–83

In the modern contractual marriage, which takes place at the desire of husband and wife, marriage and love are united.

Socialism, p. 83

MARTYRDOM

There have always been men who voluntarily renounced many pleasures and satisfactions in order to do what they considered right and moral. Men have preferred martyrdom to the renunciation of what they believed to be true. They have chosen poverty and exile because they wanted to be free in the search for truth and wisdom. All that is noblest in the progress of civilization, welfare, and enlightenment has been the

144

achievement of such men, who braved every danger and defied the tyranny of powerful kings and fanatical masses.

Omnipotent Government, p. 114

MARXISM

The essence of Marxian philosophy is this: We are right because we are the spokesmen of the rising proletarian class. Discursive reasoning cannot invalidate our teachings, for they are inspired by the supreme power that determines the destiny of mankind. Our adversaries are wrong because they lack the intuition that guides our minds.

Human Action, p. 84; p. 83

The Marxian dogma according to which socialism is bound to come "with the inexorability of a law of nature" is just an arbitrary surmise devoid of any proof.

Planning for Freedom, p. 33

Marx's economic teachings are essentially a garbled rehash of the theories of Adam Smith and, first of all, of Ricardo.

Theory and History, pp. 124–25

Marxism is a revolutionary doctrine. It expressly declares that the design of the prime mover will be accomplished by civil war. . . . The liquidation of all dissenters will establish the undisputed supremacy of the absolute eternal values. This formula for the solution of conflicts of value judgments is certainly not new. It is a device known and practiced from time immemorial. Kill the infidels! Burn the heretics! What is new is merely the fact that today it is sold to the public under the label of "science."

Theory and History, p. 51

For Marx and his parties, the interests of the individual classes are irreconcilably opposed to each other. Each class knows precisely what his class interests are and how to realize them. Therefore, there can only be warfare.

A Critique of Interventionism, p. 118

Even the most orthodox Marxians are not bold enough to support seriously its essential thesis, namely, that capitalism results in a progressive impoverishment of the wage earners.

Human Action, p. 691; p. 694

All the sophisticated syllogisms of the ponderous volumes published by Marx, Engels, and hundreds of Marxian authors cannot conceal the fact that the only and ultimate source of Marx's prophecy is an alleged inspiration by virtue of which Marx claims to have guessed the plans of the mysterious powers determining the course of history. Like Hegel, Marx was a prophet communicating to the people the revelation that an inner voice had imparted to him.

Human Action, p. 691; p. 695

The incomparable success of Marxism is due to the prospect it offers of fulfilling those dream-aspirations and dreams of vengeance which have been so deeply imbedded in the human soul from time immemorial. It promises a Paradise on earth, a Land of Heart's Desire full of happiness and enjoyment, and—sweeter still to the losers in life's game—humiliation of all who are stronger and better than the multitude. Logic and reasoning, which might show the absurdity of such dreams of bliss and revenge, are to be thrust aside. . . . It is against Logic, against Science and against the activity of thought itself.

Socialism, p. 7

The Bolshevists persistently tell us that religion is opium for the people. Marxism is indeed opium for those who might take to thinking and must therefore be weaned from it.

Socialism, p. 7

Marx and Engels never tried to refute their opponents with argument. They insulted, ridiculed, derided, slandered, and traduced them, and in the use of these methods their followers are not less expert. Their polemic is directed never against the argument of the opponent, but always against his person.

Socialism, p. 19

He did not know what to say in the planned 52nd chapter of the third volume and this embarrassment induced him to desist from finishing his great treatise. The essential dogma of the Marxian philosophy, the class conflict doctrine which he and his friend Engels had propagated for many decades, was unmasked as a flop.

Economic Freedom and Interventionism, p, 121

They have no greater perception of the essentials of economic life than the errand boy, whose only idea of the work of the entrepreneur is that he covers pieces of paper with letters and figures.

Socialism, p. 189

In its most fundamental contentions Marxism has never risen above the level of a doctrine for the soap box orator.

Socialism, p. 305

Within Marxism there is no place for free thought.

Socialism, p. 319

The Marxians' love of democratic institutions was a stratagem only, a pious fraud for the deception of the masses. Within a socialist community there is no room left for freedom. There can be no freedom of the press where the government owns every printing office. There can be no free choice of profession or trade where the government is the only employer and assigns everyone the task he must fulfill. There can be no freedom to settle where one chooses when the government has the power to fix one's place of work. There can be no real freedom of scientific research where the government owns all the libraries, archives, and laboratories and has the right to send anyone to a place where he cannot continue his investigation. There can be no freedom in art and literature where the government determines who shall create them. There can be neither freedom of conscience nor of speech where the government has the power to remove any opponent to a climate which is detrimental to his health, or to assign him duties which surpass his strength and ruin him both physically and intellectually.

Omnipotent Government, pp. 51–52

In the eyes of the Marxians, Ricardo, Freud, Bergson, and Einstein are wrong because they are bourgeois; in the eyes of the Nazis they are wrong because they are Jews.

Omnipotent Government, p. 145

MATERIAL GOODS

Strictly speaking, people do not long for tangible goods as such, but for the services which these goods are fitted to render them.

Human Action, p. 234; p. 233

In reality no food is valued solely for its nutritive power and no garment or house solely for the protection it affords against cold weather and rain. It cannot be denied that the demand for goods is widely influenced by metaphysical, religious, and ethical considerations, by aesthetic value judgments, by customs, habits, prejudice, tradition, changing fashions, and many other things.

Human Action, p. 234; p. 233

MATERIAL WELL-BEING

Notwithstanding all declarations to the contrary, the immense majority of men aim first of all at an improvement of the material conditions of well-being. They want more and better food, better homes and clothes and a thousand other amenities. They strive after abundance and health.

Human Action, p. 96; p. 96

The average American worker enjoys amenities for which Croesus, Crassus, the Medici, and Louis XIV would have envied him.

Human Action, p. 265; p. 265

The increase in per capita consumption [material well-being] in America as compared with the conditions a quarter of a century ago is not an achievement of laws and executive orders. It is an accomplishment of businessmen who enlarged the size of their factories or built new ones.

Planned Chaos, p. 15

The immense majority strives after a greater and better supply of food, clothes, homes, and other material amenities. In calling a rise in the masses' standard of living progress and improvement, economists do not espouse a mean materialism.

They simply establish the fact that people are motivated by the urge to improve the material conditions of their existence.

Human Action, pp. 193–94; p. 193

The only means to increase a nation's welfare is to increase and to improve the output of products.

Planning for Freedom, p. 6

The preservation and the further improvement of what is called "the American way of life" and "an American standard of living" depends on the maintenance and the further increase of the capital invested in American business.

Planning for Freedom, p. 92

A nation cannot prosper if its members are not fully aware of the fact that what alone can improve their conditions is more and better production. And this can only be brought about by increased saving and capital accumulation.

Planning for Freedom, pp. 92–93

There is but one means to improve the material well-being of men, viz., to accelerate the increase in capital accumulated as against population.

Planning for Freedom, p. 143

Not through war and victory but only through work can a nation create the preconditions for the well-being of its members.

Nation, State, and Economy, p. 87

MEDIA

Modern tyrants have things much easier than their predecessors. He who rules the means of exchange of ideas and of goods in the economy based on the division of labor has his rule more firmly grounded than ever an imperator before. The rotary press is easy to put into fetters, and whoever controls it need not fear the competition of the merely spoken or written word. Things were much more difficult for the Inquisition. No Phillip II could paralyze freedom of thought more severely than a modern censor. How much more efficient than the guillotine of Robespierre are the machine guns of Trotsky!

Nation, State, and Economy, p. 216

MENGER, CARL

Nazi economists wasted much time in searching the genealogical tree of Carl Menger for Jewish ancestors; they did not succeed.

Omnipotent Government, p. 147

METAPHYSICS

It is not to be denied that the loftiest theme that human thought can set for itself is reflection on ultimate questions. Whether such reflection can accomplish anything is doubtful.

Epistemological Problems of Economics, p. 49

One may hold poets, prophets, or promulgators of new values in higher esteem than scientists. But in no case is one free to confound these two fundamentally different functions.

Epistemological Problems of Economics, p. 49

Metaphysics and science perform different functions. They cannot, therefore, adopt the same procedures, nor are they alike in their goals. They can work side by side without enmity because they need not dispute each other's domain as long as they do not misconstrue their own character. A conflict arises only when one or the other attempts to overstep the boundary between them.

Epistemological Problems of Economics, p. 49

MIGRATION

The principles of freedom, which have gradually been gaining ground everywhere since the eighteenth century, gave people freedom of movement.

Nation, State, and Economy, p. 58

A nation that believes in itself and its future, a nation that means to stress the sure feeling that its members are bound to one another not merely by accident of birth but also by the common possession of a culture that is valuable above all to each of them, would necessarily be able to remain unperturbed when it saw individual persons shift to other nations.

Nation, State, and Economy, p. 76

MILITARY

The conduct of military affairs is characterized by a stubborn hostility to every attempt toward improvement.

Bureaucracy, p. 67

The military state is a state of bandits. It prefers to live on booty and tribute.

Socialism, p. 221

In proportion as armaments increased the sales of munitions plants, they reduced the sales of all other industries.

Omnipotent Government, p. 133

For all nations the necessity of being ready for defense will mean a heavy burden. Not only economic but moral and political conditions will be affected. Militarism will supplant democracy; civil liberties will vanish wherever military discipline must be supreme.

Omnipotent Government, p. 287

The characteristic feature of militarism is not the fact that a nation has a powerful army or navy. It is the paramount role assigned to the army within the political structure. Even in peacetime the army is supreme; it is the predominant factor in political life. The subjects must obey the government as soldiers must obey their superiors. Within a militarist community there is no freedom; there are only obedience and discipline.

Omnipotent Government, p. 35

MILITARY INDUSTRIAL COMPLEX

The armament industry created militarism and imperialism, however, just as little as, say, the distilleries created alcoholism or publishing houses trashy literature. The supply of weapons did not call forth the demand, but rather the other way around.

Nation, State, and Economy, p. 155

The leaders of the armament industry are not themselves bloodthirsty; they would just as gladly earn money by producing other commodities. They produce cannons and guns because demand for them exists; they would just as gladly produce peacetime articles if they could do a better business with them.

Nation, State, and Economy, p. 155

MIND

The person who has a low opinion of the mind is not the one who wants to make it free from all external regulation but rather the one who wants to control it by penal laws and machine guns.

Nation, State, and Economy, p. 215

MINORITIES

To be a member of a national minority involves multitudinous political disadvantages. The wider the functions of the political authority the more burdensome are these disadvantages.

Socialism, p. 202

Because of the enormous power that today stands at the command of the state, a national minority must expect the worst from a majority of a different nationality. As long as the state is granted the vast powers which it has today and which public opinion considers to be its right, the thought of having to live in a state whose government is in the hands of members of a foreign nationality is positively terrifying. It is frightful to live in a state in which at every turn one is exposed to persecution—masquerading under the guise of justice—by a ruling majority. It is dreadful to be handicapped even as a child in school on account of one's nationality and to be in the wrong before every judicial and administrative authority because one belongs to a national minority.

Liberalism, p. 141

MONETARY POLICY

All monetary policies encounter the difficulty that the effects of any measures taken . . . can neither be foreseen in advance, nor their nature and magnitude be determined even after they have already occurred.

The Theory of Money and Credit, p. 271

The interests of the capitalists are scarcely ever represented in monetary policy.

The Theory of Money and Credit, p. 414

MONEY

Money is regarded as the cause of theft and murder, of deception and betrayal. Money is blamed when the prostitute sells her body and when the bribed judge perverts the law. It is money against which the moralist declaims when he wishes to oppose excessive materialism.

The Theory of Money and Credit, p. 111

Money is merely the commonly used medium of exchange; it plays only an intermediary role. What the seller wants ultimately to receive in exchange for the commodities sold is other commodities. Every commodity produced is therefore a price, as it were, for other commodities produced. The situation of the producer of any commodity is improved by any increase in the production of other commodities.

Planning for Freedom, p. 66

Only the naive inflationists could believe that government could enrich mankind through fiat money.

A Critique of Interventionism, p. 23

For two hundred years the governments have interfered with the market's choice of the money medium. Even the most bigoted étatists do not venture to assert that this interference has proved beneficial.

Human Action, p. 419; p. 422

Fiat money is a money consisting of mere tokens which can neither be employed for any industrial purposes nor convey a claim against anybody.

Human Action, p. 426; p. 429

The governments alone are responsible for the spread of the superstitious awe with which the common man looks upon every bit of paper upon which the treasury or agencies which it controls have printed the magical words *legal tender.*

Human Action, pp. 444–45; p. 448

No technological computation and calculation would be possible in an environment that would not employ a generally used medium of exchange, money.

The Ultimate Foundation of Economic Science, p. 127

Money is nothing but a medium of exchange and it completely fulfills its function when the exchange of goods and services is carried on more easily with its help than would be possible to means of barter.

The Theory of Money and Credit, p. 31

Where the free exchange of goods and services is unknown, money is not wanted.

The Theory of Money and Credit, p. 41

The simple statement, that money is a commodity whose economic function is to facilitate the interchange of goods and services, does not satisfy those writers who are interested rather in the accumulation of material than in the increase of knowledge.

The Theory of Money and Credit, pp. 46–47

Money has thus become an aid that the human mind is no longer able to dispense with in making economic calculations.

The Theory of Money and Credit, p. 62

Money has no utility other than that arising from the possibility of obtaining other economic goods in exchange for it.

The Theory of Money and Credit, p. 118

The valuation of the monetary unit depends not upon the wealth of the country, but upon the ratio between the quantity of money and the demand for it, so that even the richest country may have a bad currency and the poorest country a good one.

The Theory of Money and Credit, p. 278

MONEY SUPPLY

If it were really possible to substitute credit expansion (cheap money) for the accumulation of capital goods by saving, there would not be any poverty in the world.

Planning for Freedom, p. 190

Depression is the aftermath of credit expansion.

Planning for Freedom, p. 7

If you increase the quantity of money, you bring about the lowering of the purchasing power of the monetary unit.

Economic Policy, p. 66

The quantity of money available in the whole economy is always sufficient to secure for everybody all that money does and can do.

Human Action, p. 418; p. 421

All present-day governments are fanatically committed to an easy money policy.

Human Action, p. 570; p. 572

No increase in the welfare of the members of a society can result from the availability of an additional quantity of money.

The Theory of Money and Credit, p. 102

No nation need fear at any time to have less money than it needs.

The Theory of Money and Credit, pp. 208–09

In all countries where inflation has been rapid, it has been observed that the decrease in the value of the money has occurred faster than the increase in its quantity.

The Theory of Money and Credit, p. 259

The entrepreneurs who approach banks for loans are suffering from shortage of capital; it is never shortage of money in the proper sense of the word.

The Theory of Money and Credit, p. 349

MONOPOLIES

The monopoly problem mankind has to face today is not an outgrowth of the operation of the market economy. It is a product of purposive action on the part of governments. It is not one of the evils inherent in capitalism as the demagogues trumpet. It is, on the contrary, the fruit of policies hostile to capitalism and intent upon sabotaging and destroying its operation.

Human Action, p. 363; p. 366

The widespread view that the monopolist can fix prices at will, that—in common phrase—he can dictate prices, is as erroneous as the conclusion, derived from this view, that he has in his hands the power to do whatever he likes.

Socialism, p. 344

Most cartels and trusts would never have been set up had not the governments created the necessary conditions by protectionist measures. Manufacturing and commercial monopolies owe their origin not to a tendency immanent in capitalist economy but to governmental interventionist policy directed against free trade and *laissez-faire.*

Socialism, p. 349

MYSTERY

We are still far from understanding the ultimate and most profound secret of life, the principle of the origin of organisms. Who knows whether we shall ever discover it?

Socialism, p. 259

There is within the infinite expanse of what is called the universe or nature a small field in which man's conscious conduct can influence the course of events.

The Ultimate Foundation of Economic Science, p. 11

Perhaps there are somewhere in the infinite universe beings whose minds outrank our minds to the same extent as our minds surpass those of the insects. Perhaps there will once somewhere live beings who will look upon us with the same condescension as we look upon amoebae.

The Ultimate Foundation of Economic Science, p. 17

Scientific research will never succeed in providing a full answer to what is called the riddles of the universe. It can never show how out of an inconceivable nothing emerged all that is and how one day all that exists may again disappear and the "nothing" alone will remain.

The Ultimate Foundation of Economic Science, p. 53

Man is only a tiny speck in the infinite vastness of the universe and that the whole history of mankind is but a fleeting episode in the endless flux of eternity.

The Ultimate Foundation of Economic Science, p. 125

Man's place in that part of the universe about which we can learn something is certainly modest only.

The Ultimate Foundation of Economic Science, p. 125

NATIONALISM

The older nationality principle is peaceful; it wants no war between peoples and believes that no reason for one exists.

Nation, State, and Economy, p. 43

Nationalist policies, which always begin by aiming at the ruination of one's neighbor, must, in the final analysis, lead to the ruination of all.

Liberalism, p. 144

The nationality principle above all bears no sword against members of other nations. It is directed *in tyrannos.* Therefore, above all, there is also no opposition between national and citizen-of-the-world attitudes. The idea of freedom is both national and cosmopolitan. It is revolutionary, for it wants to abolish all rule incompatible with its principles, but it is also pacifistic. What basis for war could there still be, once all peoples had been set free? Political liberalism concurs on that point with economic liberalism, which proclaims the solidarity of interests among peoples.

Nation, State, and Economy, p. 35

The further a nation goes on the road toward public control of business, the more it is forced to withdraw from the international division of labor.

Omnipotent Government, p. 281

It would be a mistake to ascribe the ascendancy of modern nationalism to human wickedness. The nationalists are not innately aggressive men; they become aggressive through their conception of nationalism. They are confronted with conditions which were unknown to the champions of the old principle of self-determination. And their etatist prejudices prevent them from finding a solution for the problems they have to face other than that provided by aggressive nationalism.

Omnipotent Government, pp. 81–82

Present-day protectionism is a necessary corollary of the domestic policy of government interference with business. Interventionism begets economic nationalism. It thus kindles the antagonism resulting in war. An abandonment of economic nationalism is not feasible if nations cling to interference with business. Free trade in international relations requires domestic free trade.

Omnipotent Government, p. 66

The nationalists of all countries have succeeded in convincing their followers that only the policies they recommend are really advantageous to the well-being of the whole nation and of all its honest citizens.

Omnipotent Government, p. 115

Aggressive nationalism is the necessary derivative of the policies of interventionism and national planning.

Human Action, p. 819; p. 823

Economic nationalism, the necessary complement of domestic interventionism, hurts the interests of foreign peoples and thus creates international conflict. It suggests the idea of amending this unsatisfactory state of affairs by war.

Human Action, p. 827; p. 831

Interventionism generates economic nationalism, and economic nationalism generates bellicosity. If men and commodities are prevented from crossing the borderlines, why should not the armies try to pave the way for them?

Human Action, p. 828; p. 832

NATURAL SCIENCES

In the realm of nature we cannot know anything about final causes, by reference to which events can be explained. But in the field of human actions there is the finality of acting men.

Men make choices. They aim at certain ends and they apply means in order to attain the ends sought.

Omnipotent Government, p. 120

Nothing could by more mistaken than the now fashionable attempt to apply the methods and concepts of the natural sciences to the solution of social problems.

Omnipotent Government, p. 120

What makes natural science possible is the power to experiment; what makes social science possible is the power to grasp or to comprehend the meaning of human action.

Money, Method, and the Market Process, p. 9

NATURE

In nature there is nothing that could be called freedom. Nature is inexorable necessity.

Planning for Freedom, p. 215

In nature there prevail irreconcilable conflicts of interest. The means of subsistence are scarce. Proliferation tends to outrun subsistence. Only the fittest plants and animals survive. The antagonism between an animal starving to death and another that snatches the food away from it is implacable.

Human Action, pp. 273–74; p. 273

It is illusory to maintain that individuals in renouncing the alleged blessings of a fabulous state of nature and entering into society have foregone some advantages and have a fair claim to be indemnified for what they have lost. The idea that anybody would have fared better under an asocial state of mankind and is wronged by the very existence of society is absurd. Thanks to the higher productivity of social cooperation the human species has multiplied far beyond the margin of subsistence offered by the conditions prevailing in ages with a rudimentary degree of the division of labor. Each man enjoys a standard of living much higher than that of his savage ancestors. The natural condition of man is extreme poverty and insecurity. It is romantic nonsense to lament the passing of the happy days of primitive barbarism.

Human Action, p. 165; p. 165

Nature is not bountiful but stingy. It has restricted the supply of all things indispensable for the preservation of human life. It has populated the world with animals and plants to whom the impulse to destroy human life and welfare is inwrought. It displays powers and elements whose operation is damaging to human life and to human endeavors to preserve it. Man's survival and well-being are an achievement of the skill with which he has utilized the main instrument with which nature has equipped him—reason.

The Anti-Capitalistic Mentality, p. 81

Men, cooperating under the system of the division of labor, have created all the wealth which the daydreamers consider as a free gift of nature.

The Anti-Capitalistic Mentality, p. 81

For the primary task of reason is to cope consciously with the limitations imposed upon man by nature, to fight against scarcity.

Human Action, p. 237; p. 236

He who does not know how to safeguard his equilibrium when surrounded by motorcycles and telephones will not find it in the jungle or dessert.

A Critique of Interventionism, p. 130

164

Love of nature and appreciation of the beauties of the landscape were foreign to the rural population. The inhabitants of the cities brought them to the countryside. It was the city-dwellers who began to appreciate the land as *nature*, while the countrymen valued it only from the point of view of its productivity for hunting, lumbering, crop raising and cattle breeding. From time immemorial the rocks and glaciers of the Alps were merely waste land in the eyes of the mountaineers. Only when the townsfolk ventured to climb the peaks, and brought money into the valleys, did they change their minds. The pioneers of mountain climbing and skiing were ridiculed by the indigenous population until they found out that they could derive gain from this eccentricity.

Human Action, p. 641; p. 645

The life of primitive man was an unceasing struggle against the scantiness of the nature-given means for sustenance. In this desperate effort to secure bare survival, many individuals and whole families, tribes, and races succumbed. Primitive man was always haunted by the specter of death from starvation. Civilization has freed us from these perils.

Human Action, p. 600; p. 602

Not shepherds, but sophisticated aristocrats and city-dwellers were the authors of bucolic poetry. Daphnis and Chloë are creations of fancies far removed from earthy concerns. No less removed from the soil is the modern political myth of the soil. It did not blossom from the moss of the forests and the loam of the fields, but from the pavements of the cities and the carpets of the salons. The farmers make use of it because they find it a practical means of obtaining political privileges which raise the prices of their products and of their farms.

Human Action, p. 641; p. 645

In Nature too, much may exist that we do not like. But we cannot change the essential character of natural events. If, for example, someone thinks—and there are some who have maintained as much—that the way in which man ingests his food, digests it, and incorporates it into his body is disgusting, one cannot argue the point with him. One must say to him: There is only this way or starvation.

Liberalism, p. 88

NAZISM

The foreign critics condemn the Nazi system as capitalist. . . . But this is one charge against the Nazis that is unfounded.

Omnipotent Government, p. 225

This is socialism in the outward guise of capitalism.

Omnipotent Government, p. 56

The mass slaughters perpetrated in the Nazi horror camps are too horrible to be adequately described by words. But they were the logical and consistent application of doctrines and policies parading as applied science and approved by some men who in a sector of the natural sciences have displayed acumen and technical skill in laboratory research.

Planned Chaos, p. 79

The doctrines of Nazism are vicious, but they do not essentially disagree with the ideologies of socialism and nationalism as approved by other peoples' public opinion. What characterized the Nazis was only the consistent application of these ideologies to the special conditions of Germany.

Human Action, p. 187; p. 187

There was no secrecy about the ambitions of the Nazis. The Nazis themselves advertised them in innumerable books and pamphlets, and in every issue of their numerous newspapers and periodicals. Nobody can reproach the Nazis with having concocted their plots clandestinely. He who had ears to hear and eyes to see could not help but know all about their aspirations.

Omnipotent Government, p. 12

The main point in the propaganda of Nazism between 1919 and 1933 was: World Jewry and Western capitalism have caused your misery; we will fight these foes, thus rendering you more prosperous.

Omnipotent Government, p. 115

Tacitus informs us that the German tribes of his day considered it clumsy and shameful to acquire with sweat what could be won by bloodshed. This is also the first moral principle of the Nazis. They despise individuals and nations eager to profit by serving other people; in their eyes robbery is the noblest way to make a living.

Omnipotent Government, p. 180

The inflation had pauperized the middle classes. The victims joined Hitler. But they did not do so because they had suffered but because they believed that Nazism would relieve them. That a man suffers from bad digestion does not explain why he consults a quack. He consults the quack because he thinks that the man will cure him. If he had other opinions, he would consult a doctor. That there was economic distress in Germany does not account for Nazism's success.

Omnipotent Government, p. 219

Hitler and his clique conquered Germany by brutal violence, by murder and crime. But the doctrines of Nazism had got hold

167

of the German mind long before then. Persuasion, not violence, had converted the immense majority of the nation to the tenets of militant nationalism. If Hitler had not succeeded in winning the race for dictatorship, somebody else would have won it.

Omnipotent Government, pp. 221–22

Nazism conquered Germany because it never encountered any adequate intellectual resistance.

Omnipotent Government, p. 222

Yet it is clear that both systems, the German and the Russian, must be considered from an economic point of view as socialist.

Omnipotent Government, p. 178

NEW DEAL

The comparatively greater prosperity of the United States is an outcome of the fact that the New Deal did not come in 1900 or 1910, but only in 1933.

Planning for Freedom, p. 136

The government embarked upon a vast scheme for restricting output, raising prices, and subsidizing the farmers. In interfering for the special benefit of the submarginal farmer it did so to the disadvantage of everyone consuming food and cotton and to the disadvantage of the taxpayer.

Omnipotent Government, p. 249

PACIFISM

To be judged quite differently from this older pacifism, which was carried along by general considerations of humanitarianism and horror of bloodshed, is the pacifism of the Enlightenment philosophy of natural law, of economic liberalism, and of political democracy, which has been cultivated since the eighteenth century. It does not arise from a sentiment that calls on the individual and the state to renounce the pursuit of their earthly interests out of thirst for fame or in hope of reward in the beyond; nor does it stand as a separate postulate without organic connection with other moral demands. Rather, pacifism here follows with logical necessity from the entire system of social life. He who, from the utilitarian standpoint, rejects the rule of some over others and demands the full right of self-determination for individuals and peoples has thereby rejected war also.

Nation, State, and Economy, pp. 85–86

All pacifism not based on a liberal economic order built on private ownership of the means of production always remains utopian.

Nation, State, and Economy, p. 94

Liberal pacifism demands peace because it considers war useless. That is a view understandable only from the standpoint of the free-trade doctrine as developed in the classical theory of Hume, Smith, and Ricardo. He who wants to prepare a lasting peace must, like Bentham, be a free-trader and a democrat and work with decisiveness for the removal of all political rule over colonies by a mother country and fight for the full freedom of movement of persons and goods. Those and no others are the preconditions of eternal peace. If one wants to make peace, then one must get rid of the possibility of conflicts between peoples. Only the ideas of liberalism and democracy have the power to do that.

Nation, State, and Economy, p. 86

PATENTS

If the government objects to monopoly prices for new inventions, it should stop granting patents.

Human Action, p. 760; p. 766

PATERNALISM

Once you begin to admit that it is the duty of the government to control your consumption of alcohol, what can you reply to those who say the control of books and ideas is much more important?

Economic Policy, p. 22

It is a fact that no paternal government, whether ancient or modern, ever shrank from regimenting its subjects' minds, beliefs, and opinions. If one abolishes man's freedom to determine his own consumption, one takes all freedoms away. The naive advocates of government interference with consumption delude themselves when they neglect what they disdainfully call the philosophical aspect of the problem. They unwittingly support the case of censorship, inquisition, religious intolerance, and the persecution of dissenters.

Human Action, p. 729; p. 734

PATRIOTISM

Patriotism is the zeal for one's own nation's welfare, flowering, and freedom.

Omnipotent Government, p. 2

The sacrifice that is demanded of the soldier serving by compulsion can be compensated only with intangible values, never with material ones.

Nation, State, and Economy, p. 166

PEACE

The goal of the domestic policy of liberalism is the same as that of its foreign policy: peace. It aims at peaceful cooperation just as much between nations as within each nation.

Liberalism, p. 105

PERVERSITY

The notions of abnormality and perversity therefore have no place in economics. It does not say that a man is perverse because he prefers the disagreeable, the detrimental, and the painful to the agreeable, the beneficial and the pleasant. It says only that he is different from other people; that he likes what others detest; that he considers useful what others want to avoid; that he takes pleasure in enduring pain which others avoid because it hurts them.

Human Action, p. 95; p. 95

PLANNED ECONOMY

The planned economy is the most rigid system of enslavement history has ever known.

Money, Method, and the Market Process, p. 282

PLATO

Plato was anxious to find a tyrant who would use his power for the realization of the Platonic ideal state. The question whether other people would like or dislike what he himself had in store for them never occurred to Plato.

The Ultimate Foundation of Economic Science, p. 95

Plato founded his utopia on the hope that a small group of perfectly wise and morally impeccable philosophers will be available for the supreme conduct of affairs.

The Ultimate Foundation of Economic Science, p. 99

POETRY

It has sometimes been asserted that there is more truth in fiction than in history. Insofar as the novel or play is looked upon as a disclosure of the author's mind, this is certainly correct. The poet always writes about himself, always analyzes his own soul.

Theory and History, p. 280

POLICE POWER

Freedom and liberty always mean freedom from police interference.

Planned Chaos, p. 64

The police officer and the fireman have no better claim to the public's gratitude than the doctors, the railroad engineers, the welders, the sailors, or the manufacturers of any useful commodity. The traffic cop has no more cause for conceit than the manufacturer of traffic lights.

Bureaucracy, p. 77

It is in the nature of every application of violence that it tends toward a transgression of the limit within which it is tolerated and viewed as legitimate. Even the best discipline cannot always prevent police officers from striking harder than circumstances require, or prison wardens from inflicting brutalities on inmates.

Omnipotent Government, p. 156

The men who are to protect the community against violent aggression easily turn into the most dangerous aggressors. They transgress their mandate. They misuse their power for the oppression of those whom they were expected to defend against oppression. The main political problem is how to prevent the police power from becoming tyrannical. This is the meaning of all the struggles for liberty.

The Ultimate Foundation of Economic Science, p. 98

POLITICAL PARTIES

He who is unfit to serve his fellow citizens wants to rule them.

Bureaucracy, p. 92

There are no longer real political parties in the old classical sense, but merely *pressure groups.*

Economic Policy, p. 96

In the United States, the two-party system of the old days is seemingly still preserved. But this is only a camouflage of the real situation. In fact, the political life of the United States . . .

is determined by the struggle and aspirations of pressure groups.

Economic Policy, p. 96

There can be no more grievous misunderstanding of the meaning and nature of liberalism than to think that it would be possible to secure the victory of liberal ideas by resorting to the methods employed today by the other political parties.

Liberalism, p. 158

All modern political parties and all modern party ideologies originated as a reaction on the part of special group interests fighting for a privileged status against liberalism.

Liberalism, p. 160

To the parties of special interests, all political questions appear exclusively as problems of political tactics. Their ultimate goal is fixed for them from the start. Their aim is to obtain, at the cost of the rest of the population, the greatest possible advantages and privileges for the groups they represent. The party platform is intended to disguise this objective and give it a certain appearance of justification, but under no circumstances to announce it publicly as the goal of party policy. The members of the party, in any case, know what their goal is; they do not need to have it explained to them. How much of it ought to be imparted to the world is, however, a purely tactical question.

Liberalism, pp. 175–76

The enemies of liberalism have branded it as the party of the special interests of the capitalists. This is characteristic of their mentality. They simply cannot understand a political ideology as anything but the advocacy of certain special privileges opposed to the general welfare.

Liberalism, p. 183

Many people complain today about the lack of creative statesmanship. However, under the predominance of interventionist ideas, a political career is open only to men who identify themselves with the interests of a pressure group. . . . Service to the short-run interests of a pressure group is not conducive to the development of those qualities which make a great statesman. Statesmanship is invariably long-run policy; but pressure groups do not bother about the long run.

Human Action, p. 866; p. 870

If our community does not beget men who have the power to make sound social principles generally acceptable, civilization is lost, whatever the system of government may be.

Omnipotent Government, p. 119

It is obvious that every constitutional system can be made to work satisfactorily when the rulers are equal to their task. The problem is to find the men fit for office.

Omnipotent Government, p. 120

No politician is any longer interested in the question whether a measure is fit to produce the ends aimed at. What alone counts for him is whether the majority of the voters favor or reject it.

The Ultimate Foundation of Economic Science, p. 94

POLITICS

The main political problem is how to prevent the rulers from becoming despots and enslaving the citizenry.

The Theory of Money and Credit, p. 454

The worst and most dangerous form of absolutist rule is that of an intolerant majority.

Theory and History, p. 67

For the charismatic leader but one thing matters: the faithful performance of his mission no matter what the means he may be forced to resort to. He is above all laws and moral precepts. What he does is always right, and what his opponents do is always wrong.

Theory and History, p. 164

Any attempt to found a party of special interests on the bias of an equal apportionment of privileges among the majority of the population would be utterly senseless. A privilege accruing to the majority ceases to be such.

Liberalism, p. 168

There is an inherent tendency in all governmental power to recognize no restraints on its operation and to extend the sphere of its dominion as much as possible. To control everything, to leave no room for anything to happen of its own accord without the interference of the authorities—this is the goal for which every ruler secretly strives.

Liberalism, p. 67

The characteristic mark of this age of dictators, wars and revolutions is its anticapitalistic bias. Most governments and political parties are eager to restrict the sphere of private initiative and free enterprise.

Planned Chaos, p. 15

The mixing of politics and business not only is detrimental to politics, as is frequently observed, but even much more so to business.

A Critique of Interventionism, p. 162

Political realism, that hodgepodge of cynicism, lack of conscience, and unvarnished selfishness.

Nation, State, and Economy, p. 69

POPULATION

The transition to capitalism is thus accompanied by two phenomena: a decline both in fertility rates and in mortality rates. The average duration of life is prolonged.

Human Action, p. 665; p. 669

Man has been able to centuple his progeny and still provide for each individual a much better life than nature offered to his nonhuman ancestors some hundred thousand years ago.

Omnipotent Government, p. 121

A return to the Middle Ages is out of the question if one is not prepared to reduce the population to a tenth or a twentieth part of its present number and, even further, to oblige every individual to be satisfied with a modicum so small as to be beyond the imagination of modern man.

Liberalism, p. 86

POSITIVISM

The sciences of human action start from the fact that man purposefully aims at ends he has chosen. It is precisely this that all brands of positivism, behaviorism, and panphysicalism want either to deny altogether or to pass over in silence.

Theory and History, p. 3

The positivists tell us that one day a new scientific discipline will emerge which will make good their promises and will describe in every detail the physical and chemical processes that produce in the body of man definite ideas. But it is evident that such a metaphysical proposition can in no way invalidate the results of the discursive reasoning of the sciences of human action.

Theory and History, p. 3

POVERTY

The riches of the rich are not the cause of the poverty of anybody; the process that makes some people rich is, on the contrary, the corollary of the process that improves many peoples' want satisfaction. The entrepreneurs, the capitalists and the technologists prosper as far as they succeed in best supplying the consumers.

The Anti-Capitalistic Mentality, p. II.1

As far as there is unhampered capitalism, there is no longer any question of poverty in the sense in which this term is applied to the conditions of a noncapitalistic society. The increase in population figures does not create supernumerary mouths, but additional hands whose employment produces additional wealth. There are no able-bodied paupers.

Human Action, p. 832; p. 836

POWER

Perhaps they think that they will exercise power for the general good, but that is what all those with power have believed. Power is evil in itself, regardless of who exercises it.

Nation, State, and Economy, p. 219

PREJUDICE

Under an unhampered market economy the appraisal of each individual's effort is detached from any personal considerations and can therefore be free both from bias and dislike. The market passes judgment on the products, not on the producers.

Bureaucracy, p. 38

PRICE

The ultimate source of the determination of prices is the value judgments of the consumers.

Human Action, p. 328; p. 331

Each individual, in buying or not buying and in selling or not selling, contributes his share to the formation of the market prices. But the larger the market is, the smaller is the weight of each individual's contribution. Thus the structure of market prices appears to the individual as a datum to which he must adjust his own conduct.

Human Action, p. 328; p. 331

It is ultimately always the subjective value judgments of individuals that determine the formation of prices.

Human Action, p. 329; p. 332

There is no such thing as prices outside the market. Prices cannot be constructed synthetically, as it were.

Human Action, p. 392; p. 395

The dangerous fact is that while government is hampered in endeavors to make a commodity cheaper by intervention, it certainly has the power to make it more expensive.

Omnipotent Government, p. 248

When people talk of a "price level," they have in mind the image of a level of a liquid which goes up or down according to the increase or decrease in its quantity, but which, like a liquid in a tank, always rises evenly. But with prices, there is no such thing as a "level." Prices do not change to the same extent at the same time. There are always prices that are changing more rapidly, rising or falling more rapidly than other prices.

Economic Policy, p. 59

PRICE CONTROL

Even capital punishment could not make price control work in the days of Emperor Diocletian and the French Revolution.

Defense, Control, and Inflation, pp. 109–10

Economics does not say that isolated government interference with the prices of only one commodity or a few commodities is unfair, bad, or unfeasible. It says that such interference produces results contrary to its purpose, that it makes conditions worse, not better, *from the point of view of the government and those backing its interference.*

Human Action, p. 758; p. 764

A government that sets out to abolish market prices is inevitably driven toward the abolition of private property; it has to recognize that there is no middle way between the system of private property in the means of production combined with free contract, and the system of common ownership of the means of production, or socialism. It is gradually forced toward compulsory production, universal obligation to labor, rationing of consumption, and, finally, official regulation of the whole of production and consumption.

The Theory of Money and Credit, p. 281

During thousands of years, in all parts of the inhabited earth, innumerable sacrifices have been made to the chimera of just and reasonable prices. Those who have offended against the laws regulating prices have been heavily punished; their property has been confiscated, they themselves have been incarcerated, tortured, put to death. The agents of etatism have certainly not been lacking in zeal and energy. But, for all this, economic affairs cannot be kept going by magistrates and policemen.

The Theory of Money and Credit, p. 282

PRIVATE PROPERTY

The program of liberalism, therefore, if condensed into a single word, would have to read: *property*, that is, private ownership of the means of production. . . . All the other demands of liberalism result from this fundamental demand.

Liberalism, p. 19

The essential teaching of liberalism is that social cooperation and the division of labor can be achieved only in a system of private ownership of the means of production, i.e., within a market society, or capitalism. All the other principles of liberalism—democracy, personal freedom of the individual, freedom of speech and of the press, religious tolerance, peace among the nations—are consequences of this basic postulate. They can be realized only within a society based on private property.

Omnipotent Government, p. 48

Private property creates for the individual a sphere in which he is free of the state. It sets limits to the operation of the authoritarian will. It allows other forces to arise side by side with and in opposition to political power. It thus becomes the basis of all those activities that are free from violent interference on the part of the state. It is the soil in which the seeds of freedom are nurtured and in which the autonomy of the individual and ultimately all intellectual and material progress are rooted.

Liberalism, pp. 67–68

If history could prove and teach us anything, it would be that private ownership of the means of production is a necessary requisite of civilization and material well-being. . . . Only nations committed to the principle of private property have risen above penury and produced science, art and literature.

Planned Chaos, p. 81

It belongs to the very essence of a society based on private ownership of the means of production that every man may work and dispose of his earnings where he thinks best.

Liberalism, p. 137

Under capitalism, private property is the consummation of the self-determination of the consumers.

Human Action, p. 680; p. 683

Social cooperation, however, can be based only on the foundation of private ownership of the means of production.

Epistemological Problems of Economics, p. 39

The continued existence of society depends upon private property, and since men have need of society, they must hold fast to the institution of private property to avoid injuring their own interests as well as the interests of everyone else. For society can continue to exist only on the foundation of private property. Whoever champions the latter champions by the same token the preservation of the social bond that unites mankind, the preservation of culture and civilization. He is an apologist and defender of society, culture, and civilization, and because he desires them as ends, he must also desire and defend the one means that leads to them, namely, private property.

Liberalism, p. 87

Governments tolerate private property when they are compelled to do so, but they do not acknowledge it voluntarily in recognition of its necessity.

Liberalism, p. 68

The "have's" do not have any more reason to support the institution of private ownership of the means of production than do the "have-not's."

Liberalism, p. 186

The truth is that every infringement of property rights and every restriction of free enterprise impairs the productivity of labor.

The Theory of Money and Credit, p. 484

PRODUCTION

Production is not an end in itself. Its purpose is to serve consumption.

On the Manipulation of Money and Credit, p. 178

The role played by man in production always consists solely in combining his personal forces with the forces of Nature in such a way that the cooperation leads to some particular desired arrangement of material. No human act of production amounts to more than altering the position of things in space and leaving the rest to Nature.

The Theory of Money and Credit, p. 97

Neither the entrepreneurs nor the farmers nor the capitalists determine what has to be produced. The consumers do that.

Human Action, p. 270; p. 270

The actual world is a world of permanent change. Population figures, tastes, and wants, the supply of factors of production and technological methods are in a ceaseless flux. In such a state of affairs there is need for a continuous adjustment of production to the change in conditions.

Bureaucracy, p. 28

The truth is that the characteristic feature of capitalism was and is mass production for the needs of the masses.

Planning for Freedom, p. 170

It is manifestly contrary to the interest of the consumers to prevent the most efficient entrepreneurs from expanding the sphere of their activities up to the limit to which the public approves of their conduct of business by buying their products.

Human Action, p. 802; p. 806

To drink coffee I do not need to own a coffee plantation in Brazil, an ocean steamer, and a coffee roasting plant, though all these means of production must be used to bring a cup of coffee to my table. Sufficient that others own these means of production and employ them for me.

Socialism, p. 31

Society is best served when the means of production are in the possession of those who know how to use them best.

Socialism, p. 66

Production is not something physical, material, and external; it is a spiritual and intellectual phenomenon.

Human Action, p. 141; p. 144

Its [production's] essential requisites are not human labor and external natural forces and things, but the decision of the mind to use these factors as means for the attainment of ends. What produces the product are not toil and trouble in themselves, but the fact that the toiling is guided by reason. The human mind alone has the power to remove uneasiness.

Human Action, pp. 141–42; pp. 141–42

PRODUCTIVITY

The increase in what is called the productivity of labor is due to the employment of better tools and machines.

The Anti-Capitalistic Mentality, p. 38

Tools and machinery are primarily not labor-saving devices, but means to increase output per unit of input.

Human Action, p. 768; p. 774

It is an illusion to believe that one can maintain productivity and reduce the division of labor.

Socialism, p. 271

In reviewing the whole history of mankind from the early beginnings of civilization up to our age, it makes sense to establish in general terms the fact that the productivity of human labor has been multiplied, for indeed the members of a civilized nation produce today much more than their ancestors did.

Human Action, No Entry; pp. 607–08

The productivity of social cooperation surpasses in every respect the sum total of the production of isolated individuals.

Epistemological Problems of Economics, p. 43

The concept of productivity is altogether subjective; it can never provide the starting-point for an objective criticism.

Liberalism, p. 65

PROFITEERS

The epithet profiteer is the expression of an arbitrary judgment of value. There is no other standard available for the distinction between profiteering and earning fair profits than that provided by the censor's personal envy and resentment.

Planning for Freedom, p. 128

PROFIT AND LOSS

Profit is the pay-off of successful action. It cannot be defined without reference to valuation. It is a phenomenon of valuation and has no direct relation to physical and other phenomena of the external world.

Human Action, p. 393; p. 396

Profit is a product of the mind, of success in anticipating the future state of the market. It is a spiritual and intellectual phenomenon.

Planning for Freedom, p. 120

The entrepreneur profits to the extent he has succeeded in serving the consumers better than other people have done.

Human Action, p. 380; p. 383

Profit is the reward for the best fulfillment of some voluntarily assumed duties. It is the instrument that makes the masses supreme.

Bureaucracy, p. 88

Profits and loss withdraw the material factors of production from the hands of the inefficient and convey them into the hands of the more efficient.

Planning for Freedom, p. 16

There would not be any profits but for the eagerness of the public to acquire the merchandise offered for sale by the successful entrepreneur, but the same people who scramble for these articles vilify the businessman and call his profit ill-got.

Planning for Freedom, p. 122

It is precisely the necessity of making profits and avoiding losses that gives to the consumers a firm hold over the entrepreneurs and forces them to comply with the wishes of the people.

Planning for Freedom, p. 134

There is no reason why capitalists and entrepreneurs should be ashamed of earning profits.

Planning for Freedom, p. 146

The elimination of profit, whatever methods may be resorted to for its execution, must transform society into a senseless jumble. It would create poverty for all.

Planning for Freedom, p. 149

Profit tells the entrepreneur that the consumers approve of his ventures; loss, that they disapprove.

Human Action, p. 701; p. 705

Profits are the driving force of the market economy. The greater the profits, the better the needs of the consumers are supplied. For profits can only be reaped by removing discrepancies between the demands of the consumers and the previous state of productions activities. He who serves the public best, makes the highest profits.

Human Action, p. 805; p. 809

It is not the fault of the entrepreneurs that the consumers—the people, the common man—prefer liquor to Bibles and detective stories to serious books, and that governments prefer guns to butter. The entrepreneur does not make greater profits in selling "bad" things than in selling "good" things. His profits are the greater the better he succeeds in providing the consumers with those things they ask for most intensely.

Human Action, p. 297; pp. 299–300

The dividends of corporations are popularly called profits. Actually they are interest on the capital invested plus that part of profits that is not ploughed back into the enterprise. If the enterprise does not operate successfully, either no dividends are paid or the dividends contain only interest on the whole or a part of the capital.

Human Action, No Entry; p. 300

PROGRESS

It is not true that human conditions must always improve, and that a relapse into very unsatisfactory modes of life, penury and barbarism is impossible.

Planning for Freedom, p. 177

There is no evidence that social evolution must move steadily upwards in a straight line. Social standstill and social retrogression are historical facts which we cannot ignore. World history is the graveyard of dead civilizations.

Socialism, p. 275

What is called economic progress is the joint effect of the activities of the three progressive groups . . . the savers, the scientist-inventors, and the entrepreneurs, operating in a market economy.

The Ultimate Foundation of Economic Science, p. 127

Whoever preaches the return to simple forms of the economic organization of society ought to keep in mind that only our type of economic system offers the possibility of supporting in the style to which we have become accustomed today the number of people who now populate the earth. A return to the Middle Ages means the extermination of many hundreds of millions of people.

Liberalism, p. 189

It is true that all this straining and struggling to increase their standard of living does not make men any happier. Nevertheless, it is in the nature of man continually to strive for an improvement in his material condition. If he is forbidden the satisfaction of this aspiration, he becomes dull and brutish. The masses will not listen to exhortations to be moderate and contented; it may be that the philosophers who preach such admonitions are laboring under a serious self-delusion. If one tells people that their fathers had it much worse, they answer that they do not know why they should not have it still better.

Liberalism, p. 190

Men always strive for an improvement in their conditions and always will. This is man's inescapable destiny.

Liberalism, p. 190

PROGRESSIVES

The "progressives" who today masquerade as "liberals" may rant against "fascism"; yet it is their policy that paves the way for Hitlerism.

Interventionism, p. 88

PROHIBITION

Mankind does not drink alcohol because there are breweries, distilleries, and vineyards; men brew beer, distill spirits, and grow grapes because of the demand for alcoholic drinks.

Socialism, p. 403

PROSPERITY

A higher standard of living also brings about a higher standard of culture and civilization.

Economic Policy, p. 89

Government cannot make man richer, but it can make him poorer.

A Critique of Interventionism, p. 23

The very existence of a comparatively great number of invalids is, however paradoxical, a characteristic mark of civilization and material well-being. Provision for those invalids who lack mean of sustenance and are not taken care of by their next of kin has long been considered a work of charity.

Human Action, p. 833; p. 837

PROSTITUTION

Since its appearance the view that prostitution is a product of capitalism has gained ground enormously. And as, in addition, preachers still complain that the good old morals have decayed, and accuse modern culture of having led to loose living, everyone is convinced that all sexual wrongs represent a symptom of decadence peculiar to our age.

Socialism, p. 92

PROTECTIONISM

A capitalist world organized on liberal principles knows no separate "economic" zones. In such a world, the whole of the earth's surface forms a single economic territory.

Liberalism, p. 113

Economic nationalism is incompatible with durable peace. Yet economic nationalism is unavoidable where there is government interference with business. Protectionism is indispensable where there is no domestic free trade. Where there is government interference with business, free trade even in the short run would frustrate the aims sought by the various interventionist measures.

Human Action, p. 682; p. 686

The philosophy of protectionism is a philosophy of war. The wars of our age are not at variance with popular economic doctrines; they are, on the contrary, the inescapable result of a consistent application of these doctrines.

Human Action, p. 683; p. 687

Government does not have the power to encourage one branch of production except by curtailing other branches. It withdraws the factors of production from those branches in which the unhampered market would employ them and directs them into other branches.

Human Action, p. 737; p. 744

The slogan "Away with foreign goods!" would lead us, if we accepted all its implications, to abolish the division of labor altogether. For the principle that makes the *international* division of labor seem advantageous is precisely the principle which recommends division of labor in any circumstances.

Socialism, p. 288

Protectionism and autarky always result in shifting production from the centers where conditions are more favorable— i.e., from where the output for the same amount of physical input is higher—to centers where they are less favorable. The more productive resources remain unused while the less productive are utilized. The effect is a general drop in the productivity of human effort, and thereby a lowering of the standard of living all over the world.

Omnipotent Government, p. 73

People favor discrimination and privileges because they do not realize that they themselves are consumers and as such must foot the bill. In the case of protectionism, for example, they believe that only the foreigners against whom the import duties discriminate are hurt. It is true the foreigners are hurt, but not they alone: the consumers who must pay higher prices suffer with them.

Omnipotent Government, p. 183

In the long run there cannot be such a thing as "moderate" protectionism. If people regard imports as an injury, they will not stop anywhere on the way toward autarky. Why tolerate an evil if there seems to be a way to get rid of it?

Omnipotent Government, p. 250

From the purely economic point of view nothing speaks against free trade and everything against protectionism.

Nation, State, and Economy, p. 64

Hunger and anarchy—that is the result of the protectionist policy.

Nation, State, and Economy, p. 75

Every restriction of trade creates vested interests that are from then onward opposed to its removal.

The Theory of Money and Credit, p. 288

PUBLIC DEBT

He who invested his funds in bonds issued by the government and its subdivisions was no longer subject to the inescapable laws of the market and to the sovereignty of the consumers. He was no longer under the necessity of investing his funds in such a way that they would best serve the wants and needs of the consumers.

Human Action, p. 226; p. 225

Income no longer stemmed from the process of supplying the wants of the consumers in the best possible way, but from the taxes levied by the state's apparatus of compulsion and coercion. He was no longer a servant of his fellow citizens, subject to their sovereignty; he was a partner of the government which ruled the people and exacted tribute from them.

Human Action, p. 226; p. 225

The public debt embodies claims of people who have in the past entrusted funds to the government against all those who are daily producing new wealth. It burdens the producing strata for the benefit of another part of the people.

Human Action, p. 229n; p. 228n

The most popular of these doctrines is crystallized in the phrase: A public debt is no burden because we owe it to ourselves. If this were true, then the wholesale obliteration of the public debt would be an innocuous operation, a mere act of bookkeeping and accountancy.

Human Action, p. 229n; p. 228n

Policies of long-term irredeemable and perpetual loans . . . offered to the citizen an opportunity to put his wealth in safety and to enjoy a stable income secure against all vicissitudes. It opened a way to free the individual from the necessity of risking and acquiring his wealth and his income anew each day in the capitalist market.

Human Action, p. 226; p. 225

The financial history of the last century shows a steady increase in the amount of public indebtedness. Nobody believes that the states will eternally drag the burden of these interest payments. It is obvious that sooner or later all these debts will be liquidated in some way or other, but certainly not by payment of interest and principal according to the terms of the contract.

Human Action, p. 228; p. 227

PUBLIC OPINION

No ruler who lacks the gift of persuasion can stay in office long; it is the indispensable condition of government. It would be an idle illusion to assume that any government, no matter how good, could lastingly do without public consent.

Omnipotent Government, p. 119

The flowering of human society depends on two factors: the intellectual power of outstanding men to conceive sound social and economic theories, and the ability of these or other men to make these ideologies palatable to the majority.

Human Action, p. 860; p. 864

In the long run no government can maintain itself in power if it does not have public opinion behind it, i.e., if those governed are not convinced that the government is good.

Liberalism, p. 41

History provides an abundance of striking examples to show that, in the long run, even the most ruthless policy of repression does not suffice to maintain a government in power.

Liberalism, p. 45

Only a group that can count on the consent of the governed can establish a lasting regime. Whoever wants to see the world governed according to his own ideas must strive for domination over men's minds. It is impossible, in the long run, to subject men against their will to a regime that they reject.

Liberalism, p. 46

The minority that desires to see its ideas triumph must strive by intellectual means to become the majority.

Liberalism, p. 59

If public opinion is ultimately responsible for the structure of government, it is also the agency that determines whether there is freedom or bondage. There is virtually only one factor that has the power to make people unfree—tyrannical public opinion. The struggle for freedom is ultimately not resistance to autocrats or oligarchs but resistance to the despotism of public opinion.

Theory and History, pp. 66–67

The truth is that most people lack the intellectual ability and courage to resist a popular movement, however pernicious and ill-considered.

Planned Chaos, p. 88

The masses favor socialism because they trust the socialist propaganda of the intellectuals. The intellectuals, not the populace, are molding public opinion.

Planned Chaos, p. 90

Governments cannot free themselves from the pressure of public opinion. They cannot rebel against the preponderance of generally accepted ideologies, however fallacious. But this does not excuse the officeholders who could resign rather than carry out policies disastrous for the country.

Human Action, p. 787; p. 793

In the long run there cannot be any such thing as an unpopular system of government.

Human Action, p. 859; p. 863

The supremacy of public opinion determines not only the singular role that economics occupies in the complex of thought and knowledge. It determines the whole process of human history.

Human Action, p. 859; p. 863

The masses, the hosts of common men, do not conceive any ideas, sound or unsound. They only choose between the ideologies developed by the intellectual leaders of mankind. But their choice is final and determines the course of events. If they prefer bad doctrines, nothing can prevent disaster.

Human Action, p. 860; p. 864

PUNISHMENT

Punishment should not be vindictive or retaliatory. The criminal has incurred the penalties of the law, but not the hate and sadism of the judge, the policemen, and every lynch-thirsty mob.

Liberalism, p. 58

PURCHASING POWER

The money prices of today are linked with those of yesterday and before, and with those of tomorrow and after.

The Theory of Money and Credit, p. 130

An increase in the purchasing power of money is disadvantageous to the debtor and advantageous to the creditor; a decrease in its purchasing power has the contrary significance.

The Theory of Money and Credit, p. 229

RACES

Nation and race do not coincide; there is no nation of pure blood. All peoples have arisen from a mixture of races.

Nation, State, and Economy, p. 10

The beginnings of trade make understanding necessary between members of different tribes.

Nation, State, and Economy, p. 21

If one does not wish to aggravate artificially the friction that must arise from this living together of different groups, one must restrict the state to just those tasks that it alone can perform.

Liberalism, pp. 117–18

Let us not forget that the actual menace to our civilization does not originate from a conflict between the white and colored races but from conflict among the various peoples of Europe and of European ancestry.

Omnipotent Government, p. 107

The fundamental discrepancies in worldview and patterns of behavior do not correspond to differences in race, nationality or class affiliation. There is hardly any greater divergence in value judgments than that between ascetics and those eager to enjoy life lightheartedly.

Human Action, p. 87; p. 87

It is neither "natural" nor "necessary" that the members of the same race or the inhabitants of the same country cooperate with one another more closely than with members of other races or inhabitants of other countries. The ideas of race solidarity and racial hatred are no less ideas than any other ideas, and only where they are accepted by the individuals do they result in corresponding action.

The Ultimate Foundation of Economic Science, p. 81

RAILROADS

In the United States the competition to the railroads—in the form of busses, automobiles, trucks, and airplanes—has caused the railroads to suffer and to be almost completely defeated, as far as passenger transportation is concerned.

Economic Policy, p. 5

RATIONAL ACTION

The fundamental thesis of rationalism is unassailable. Man is a rational being; that is, his actions are guided by reason.

Theory and History, p. 269

Rational and irrational always mean: reasonable or not from the point of view of the ends sought. There is no such thing as absolute rationality or irrationality.

Omnipotent Government, p. 113

The assertion that there is irrational action is always rooted in an evaluation of a scale of values different from our own. Whoever says that irrationality plays a role in human action is merely saying that his fellow men behave in a way that he does not consider correct.

Epistemological Problems of Economics, p. 33

Rational conduct means that man, in face of the fact that he cannot satisfy all his impulses, desires, and appetites, forgoes the satisfaction of those which he considers less urgent.

Human Action, pp. 171–72; p. 172

Action is, by definition, always rational. One is unwarranted in calling goals of action irrational simply because they are not worth striving for from the point of view of one's own valuations.

Epistemological Problems of Economics, p. 35

REALITY

Life consists in adjusting oneself to actual conditions and in taking account of things as they really are, not as one would wish them to be.

Omnipotent Government, p. 13

Every enterprise has to adapt itself to the given situation, and not reckon on the situation it would like to be given.

Epistemological Problems of Economics, p. 229

One of the fundamental facts of all social life, which all reformers must take into account, is that men have their own thoughts and their own wills.

Socialism, p. 183

The cognizance of reality is a sad experience. It teaches the limits on the satisfaction of one's wishes. Only reluctantly does man resign himself to the insight that there are things, viz., the whole complex of all causal relations between events, which wishful thinking cannot alter.

Human Action, p. 858; p. 862

We must see conditions as they really are, not as we want them to be.

Omnipotent Government, p. 259

Most men endure the sacrifice of the intellect more easily than the sacrifice of their daydreams. They cannot bear that their utopias should run aground on the unalterable necessities of human existence. What they yearn for is another reality different from the one given in this world. . . . They wish to be free of a universe of whose order they do not approve.

Epistemological Problems of Economics, p. 200

REASON

Life and reality are neither logical nor illogical; they are simply given.

Austrian Economics: An Anthology, p. 156

Man has only one tool to fight error: reason.

Human Action, p. 187; p. 187

Logic is consistent in every science.

A Critique of Interventionism, p. 86

The only statement that can be predicated with regard to reason is that it is the mark that distinguishes man from animals and has brought about everything that is specifically human.

Human Action, p. 91; p. 91

Abstract thought is independent of the wishes which move the thinker and of the aims for which he strives.

Socialism, p. 317

The wish is father to the *thought,* says a figure of speech. What it means is that the wish is the father of *faith.*

Socialism, p. 317n

It is vain to object that life and reality are not logical. Life and reality are neither logical nor illogical; they are simply given. But logic is the only tool available to man for the comprehension of both.

Human Action, pp. 67–68; p. 67

Man uses reason in order to choose between the incompatible satisfactions of conflicting desires.

Human Action, p. 173; p. 174

Reason is man's particular and characteristic feature. There is no need for praxeology to raise the question whether reason is a suitable tool for the cognition of ultimate and absolute truth. It deals with reason only as far as it enables man to act.

Human Action, p. 177; p. 177

Logical thinking and real life are not two separate orbits. Logic is for man the only means to master the problems of reality.

Human Action, p. 185; p. 185

The proof of a theory is in its reasoning, not in its sponsorship.

The Theory of Money and Credit, p. 99

Not everything that exists today is reasonable; but this does not mean that everything that does not exist is sensible.

Interventionism, p. 89

What mankind needs today is liberation from the rule of nonsensical slogans and a return to sound reasoning.

Interventionism, p. 90

Reason is the main resource of man in his struggle for survival.

Omnipotent Government, p. 121

The Enlightenment did not put its hopes upon the more or less accidental emergence of well-intentioned rulers and provident sages. Its optimism concerning mankind's future was founded upon the double faith in the goodness of man and in his rational mind.

The Historical Setting of the Austrian School, p. 34

Reason is man's foremost equipment in the biological struggle for the preservation and expansion of his existence and survival. It would not have any function and would not have developed at all in the fool's paradise.

Money, Method, and the Market Process, p. 35

RECOVERY

Every country can experience the same "miracle" of economic recovery, although I must insist that economic recovery does *not* come from a miracle; it comes from the adoption of—and is the result of—sound economic policies.

Economic Policy, p. 15

REGRET

Nothing is more useless than complaining over errors that can no longer be rectified, nothing more vain than regret.

Nation, State, and Economy,

REGULARITY

If there were no regularity, nothing could be learned from experience.

The Ultimate Foundation of Economic Science, p. 21

It would be vain to search for a rule if there were no regularity.

The Ultimate Foundation of Economic Science, p. 22

In the etatist state entrepreneurs are at the mercy of officialdom. Officials enjoy discretion to decide questions on which the existence of every firm depends. They are practically free to ruin any entrepreneur they want to. They had the power not only to silence these objectors but even to force them to contribute to the party funds of nationalism.

Omnipotent Government, p. 132

RELIGION

To the believer, religion brings consolation and courage; it enables him to see himself as a thread in the fabric of eternal life, it assigns to him a place in the imperishable plan of a world creator, and places him beyond time and space, old age and death, high in the celestial pastures.

Socialism, p. 84

Although some intolerance, bigotry, and lust for persecution is still left in religious matters, it is unlikely that religious passion will kindle wars in the near future. The aggressive spirit of our age stems from another source, from endeavors to make the state totalitarian and to deprive the individual of autonomy.

Theory and History, p. 64

It is justifiable if ethics and religion tell people that they ought to make better use of the well-being that capitalism brings them. . . . But it is irresponsible to condemn one social system and to recommend its replacement by another system without having fully investigated the economic consequences of each.

Theory and History, p. 343

The churches are right to lament the destitution of the masses in the economically backward countries. But they are badly mistaken when they assume that anything can wipe out the poverty of these wretched people but unconditional adoption of the system of profit-seeking big business, that is, mass production for the satisfaction of the needs of the many.

Theory and History, pp. 343–44

Metaphysics and theology are not, as the positivists pretend, products of an activity unworthy of *Homo sapiens,* remnants of mankind's primitive age that civilized people ought to discard. They are a manifestation of man's unappeasable craving for knowledge.

The Ultimate Foundation of Economic Science, p. 120

Liberalism limits its concern entirely and exclusively to earthly ife and earthly endeavor. The kingdom of religion, on the other hand, is not of this world. Thus, liberalism and religion could both exist side by side without their spheres' touching. . . . Liberalism proclaims tolerance for every religious faith and every metaphysical belief, not out of indifference for these "higher" things, but from the conviction that the assurance of peace within society must take precedence over everything and everyone.

Liberalism, pp. 55–56

It is true that utilitarianism and liberalism postulate the attainment of the greatest possible productivity of labor as the first and most important goal of policy. But they in no way do this out of misunderstanding of the fact that human existence does not exhaust itself in material pleasures. . . . Not out of irreligiosity do they demand religious freedom but out of deepest intimacy of religious feeling, which wants to make inner experience free from every raw influence of outward power.

Nation, State, and Economy, p. 215

RETREATISM

It is a sickly weakness of nerves that urges one to seek harmonious personality growth in past ages and remote places.

A Critique of Interventionism, p. 130

There are, after all, not many people who are prepared to renounce light-heartedly the fruits of culture, however much they may despise them in thought and abuse them in words, few who are willing to return without more ado to the way of life of the deer and the stag.

Socialism, p. 365

If the diligence of modern industry were replaced by the contemplative life of the past, unnumbered millions would be doomed to death by starvation.

Socialism, p. 396

REVOLUTION

The citizen must not be so narrowly circumscribed in his activities that, if he thinks differently from those in power, his only choice is either to perish or to destroy the machinery of state.

Liberalism, p. 59

No physical violence and compulsion can possibly force a man against his will to remain in the status of the ward of a hegemonic order. What violence or the threat of violence brings about is a state of affairs in which subjection as a rule is considered more desirable than rebellion. Faced with the choice between the consequences of obedience and of disobedience, the ward prefers the former and thus integrates himself into the hegemonic bond. Every new command places this choice before him again. In yielding again and again he himself contributes his share to the continuous existence of the hegemonic societal body.

Human Action, p. 197; p. 196

The majority has the power to do away with an unpopular government and uses this power whenever it becomes convinced that its own welfare requires it. In the long run there is no such thing as an unpopular government. Civil war and revolution are the means by which the discontented majorities overthrow rulers and methods of government which do not suit them.

Human Action, pp. 149–150; pp. 149–150

Though a tyrant may temporarily rule through a minority if this minority is armed and the majority is not, in the long run a minority cannot keep the majority in subservience. The oppressed will rise in rebellion and cast off the yoke of tyranny.

Human Action, p. 189; p. 189

Violent resistance against the power of the state is the last resort of the minority in its effort to break loose from the oppression of the majority. The minority that desires to see its ideas triumph must strive by intellectual means to become the majority.

Liberalism, p. 59

RICH AND POOR

The private life of a modern entrepreneur or executive differs much less from that of his employees than, centuries ago, the life of a feudal landlord differed from that of his serfs.

Omnipotent Government, p. 117

It may indeed be true that the liberal economic order permits great differences in income, but that in no way involves exploitation of the poor by richer people. What the rich have they have not taken away from the poor; their surplus could not be more or less redistributed to the poor in the socialist society, since in that society it would not be produced at all.

Nation, State, and Economy, p. 184

It is untrue that some are poor because others are rich. If an order of society in which incomes were equal replaced the capitalist order, everyone would become poorer.

Socialism, p. 394

RISK

All economic activity is based upon an uncertain future. It is therefore bound up with risk. It is essentially speculation.

Socialism, p. 181

There is no such thing as a safe investment. If capitalists were to behave in the way the risk fable describes and were to strive after what they consider to be the safest investment, their conduct would render this line of investment unsafe and they would certainly lose their input. For the capitalist there is no means of evading the law of the market that makes it imperative for the investor to comply with the wishes of the consumers and to produce all that can be produced under the given state of capital supply, technological knowledge, and the valuations of the consumers.

Human Action, p. 806; p. 810

There is no such thing as independence of the vicissitudes of the market.

Human Action, p. 806; p. 810

The fact that a capitalist as a rule does not concentrate his investments, both in common stock and in loans, in one enterprise or one branch of business, but prefers to spread out his funds among various classes of investment, does not suggest that he wants to reduce his "gambling risk." He wants to improve his chances of earning profits.

Human Action, p. 806; p. 810

Estimates of future volume of production, future sales, future costs, or future profits or losses are not facts, but speculative anticipations. There are no facts about future profits.

Human Action, p. 812; p. 816

ROBINSON, JOAN

Once the socialist regime is "sufficiently secure to risk criticism," Miss Joan Robinson, the eminent representative of the British neo-Cambridge school, is kind enough to promise us, "even independent philharmonic societies" will be allowed to exist. Thus the liquidation of all dissenters is the condition that will bring us what the communists call freedom.

Liberty and Property, p. 15

ROMAN EMPIRE

The Roman Empire crumbled to dust because it lacked the spirit of liberalism and free enterprise. The policy of interventionism and its political corollary, the Führer principle, decomposed the mighty empire as they will by necessity always disintegrate and destroy any social entity.

Human Action, p. 763; p. 769

ROMANTICISM

Romanticism is man's revolt against reason, as well as against the condition under which nature has compelled him to live. The romantic is a daydreamer; he easily manages in imagination to disregard the laws of logic and of nature. . . . He has a grudge against reality because it is not like the dream world he has created. He hates work, economy, and reason.

Socialism, p. 419

It was writers of this class who introduced as literary figures the bloodsucking capitalist entrepreneur and the noble proletarian. To them the rich man is in the wrong because he is rich, and the poor in the right because he is poor.

Socialism, p. 420

The romantic longing for wild adventures, for quarreling and freedom from external restraint, is itself only a sign of inner emptiness; it clings to the superficial and does not strive for depth.

Nation, State, and Economy, pp. 212–13

The romantic revolt against logic and science does not limit itself to the sphere of social phenomena. . . . It is a revolt against our entire culture and civilization.

Epistemological Problems of Economics, p. 200

ROTHBARD, MURRAY

Dr. Rothbard is already well known as the author of several excellent monographs. Now, as the result of many years of sagacious and discerning meditation, he joins the ranks of eminent economists by publishing a voluminous work, a systematic treatise on economics.

Economic Freedom and Interventionism, p. 155

Now such a book as *Man, Economy, and State* offers to every intelligent man an opportunity to obtain reliable information concerning the great controversies and conflicts of our age. It is certainly not easy reading and asks for the utmost exertion of one's attention. But there are no shortcuts to wisdom.

Economic Freedom and Interventionism, p. 158

RULE OF LAW

The State is the only institution entitled to apply coercion and compulsion and to inflict harm upon individuals. This tremendous power cannot be abandoned to the discretion of some men, however competent and clever they may deem themselves. It is necessary to restrict its application. This is the task of the laws.

Bureaucracy, p. 76

The alternative to the rule of law is the rule of despots.

Bureaucracy, p. 76

It is the social function of the laws to curb the arbitrariness of the police. The rule of law restricts the arbitrariness of the officers as much as possible. It strictly limits their discretion and thus assigns to the citizens a sphere in which they are free to act without being frustrated by government interference.

Planned Chaos, pp. 63–64

It is the rule of law alone which hinders the rulers from turning themselves into the worst gangsters.

Planned Chaos, p. 64

Classical liberalism regarded those laws best that afforded the least discretionary power to executive authorities, thus avoiding arbitrariness and abuse. The modern state seeks to expand its discretionary power—everything is to be left to the discretion of officials.

A Critique of Interventionism, pp. 31–32

A state whose chiefs recognize but one rule, to do whatever seems at the moment to be expedient in their eyes, is a state without law. It does not make any difference whether or not these tyrants are "benevolent."

Omnipotent Government, p. 46

RUSSIA

Not the Russian armies, but the communist ideologies threaten the West.

Planned Chaos, p. 50

The Russian pattern of socialism is purely bureaucratic. All economic enterprises are departments of the government, like the administration of the army or the postal system. Every plant, shop, or farm stands in the same relation to the superior central organization as does a post office to the office of the postmaster general.

Omnipotent Government, p. 56

In Russia socialism certainly is not a movement of the immense majority. That it claims to be a movement in the interest of the immense majority is nothing special; all movements have claimed that. It is certain that the rule of the Bolsheviks in Russia rests just as much on possession of the government apparatus as the rule of the Romanovs once did.

Nation, State, and Economy, p. 204

Whether or not the Russian people are to discard the Soviet system is for them to settle among themselves. The land of the knout and the prison-camp no longer poses a threat to the world today. With all their will to war and destruction, the Russians are no longer capable seriously of imperiling the peace of Europe. One may therefore safely let them alone. The only thing that needs to be resisted is any tendency on our part to support or promote the destructionist policy of the Soviets.

Liberalism, p. 154

This is not to say, either, that Americans or Europeans ought to be prevented from visiting Russia if they are attracted to it. Let them view at first hand, at their own risk and on their own responsibility, the land of mass murder and mass misery. Nor does this mean that capitalists ought to be prevented from granting loans to the Soviets or otherwise to invest capital in Russia. If they are foolish enough to believe that they will ever see any part of it again, let them make the venture.

Liberalism, p. 153

RUSSIAN REVOLUTION

The real significance of the Lenin revolution is to be seen in the fact that it was the bursting forth of the principle of unrestricted violence and oppression. It was the negation of all the political ideals that had for three thousand years guided the evolution of Western civilization.

Planned Chaos, p. 63

SANCTIONS

There can be neither effective political cooperation nor solidarity and collective security among nations fighting each other in the economic sphere.

Omnipotent Government, p. 265

SAVINGS

The only source of the generation of additional capital goods is saving. If all the goods produced are consumed, no new capital comes into being.

The Anti-Capitalistic Mentality, p. 84

Capital is not a free gift of God or of nature. It is the outcome of a provident restriction of consumption on the part of man. It is created and increased by saving and maintained by the abstention from dissaving.

The Anti-Capitalistic Mentality, p. 84

At the outset of every step forward on the road to a more plentiful existence is saving—the provisionment of products that makes it possible to prolong the average period of time elapsing between the beginning of the production process and its turning out of a product ready for use and consumption. . . . Without saving and capital accumulation there could not be any striving toward nonmaterial ends.

Human Action, No Entry; p. 260

The most ingenious technological inventions would be practically useless if the capital goods required for their utilization had not been accumulated by saving.

The Anti-Capitalistic Mentality, p. 39

We are the lucky heirs of our fathers and forefathers whose saving has accumulated the capital goods with the aid of which we are working today. We favorite children of the age of electricity still derive advantage from the original saving of the primitive fishermen who, in producing the first nets and canoes, devoted a part of their working time to provision for a remoter future.

Human Action, p. 489; p. 492

SAY'S LAW

With regard to economic goods there can never be *absolute* overproduction.

Planning for Freedom, p. 65

With regard to economic goods there can be only *relative* overproduction. . . . The attempts to explain the general depression of trade by referring to an allegedly general over-production are therefore fallacious.

Planning for Freedom, p. 65

Say emerged victoriously from his polemics with Malthus and Sismondi. He proved his case, while adversaries could not prove theirs. Henceforth, during the whole rest of the nine-teenth century, the acknowledgement of the truth contained in Say's Law was the distinctive mark of an economist.

Planning for Freedom, p. 67

Keynes did not refute Say's Law. He rejected it emotionally, but he did not advance a single tenable argument to invalidate its rationale.

Planning for Freedom, p. 70

SCARCITY

The available supply of every commodity is limited. If it were not scarce with regard to the demand of the public, the thing in question would not be considered an economic good, and no price would be paid for it.

Human Action, p. 356; p. 359

SCHILLER, FREDERICK

The poems, plays, and other writings of Frederick Schiller are from beginning to end a hymn to liberty. Every word written by Schiller was a blow to the old political system of Germany; his works were fervently greeted by nearly all Germans who read books or frequented the theater.

Omnipotent Government, p. 19

SCIENCE

Science is competent to establish what *is*. It can never dictate what ought to be.

Planned Chaos, p. 30

There are no laboratory experiments in human action.

Economic Policy, p. 35

Science does not give us absolute and final certainty. It only gives us assurance within the limits of our mental abilities and the prevailing state of scientific thought. A scientific system is but one station in an endlessly progressing search for knowledge. It is necessarily affected by the insufficiency inherent in every human effort. But to acknowledge these facts does not mean that present-day economics is backward. It merely means that economics is a living thing—and to live implies both imperfection and change.

Human Action, p. 7; p. 7

What matters is not whether a doctrine is new, but whether it is sound.

Planning for Freedom, p. 53

No science can avoid abstract concepts, and he who abhors them should stay away from science and see whether and how he can go through life without them.

A Critique of Interventionism, p. 89

There are fads and fashions in the treatment of scientific problems and in the terminology of the scientific language.

The Ultimate Foundation of Economic Science, p. 69

What life and death are eludes its grasp.

Epistemological Problems of Economics, p. 44

One has to recognize that science is not metaphysics, and certainly not mysticism; it can never bring us the illumination and the satisfaction experienced by one enraptured in ecstasy. Science is sobriety and clarity of conception, not intoxicated vision.

Epistemological Problems of Economics, p. 46

Whether we see the greatest value in wisdom or in action, in neither case may we scorn science. It alone shows us the way both to knowledge and to action. Without it our existence would be only vegetative.

Epistemological Problems of Economics, p. 46

Science is universally human, and not limited by nationality, bound to a particular time, or contingent upon any social class.

Epistemological Problems of Economics, p. 152

Science cannot go beyond its own sphere. It must limit itself to the development of our system of knowledge and with its help undertake the logical elaboration of experience.

Epistemological Problems of Economics, p. 201

SECESSION

A nation, therefore, has no right to say to a province: You belong to me, I want to take you. A province consists of its inhabitants. If anybody has a right to be heard in this case it is these inhabitants. Boundary disputes should be settled by plebiscite.

Omnipotent Government, p. 90

To the princely principle of subjecting just as much land as obtainable to one's own rule, the doctrine of freedom opposes the principle of the right of self-determination of peoples, which follows necessarily from the principle of the rights of man. No people and no part of a people shall be held against its will in a political association that it does not want.

Nation, State, and Economy, p. 34

Liberalism knows no conquests, no annexations; just as it is indifferent towards the state itself, so the problem of the size of the state is unimportant to it. It forces no one against his will into the structure of the state. Whoever wants to emigrate is not held back. When a part of the people of the state wants to drop out of the union, liberalism does not hinder it from doing so. Colonies that want to become independent need only do so. The nation as an organic entity can be neither increased nor reduced by changes in states; the world as a whole can neither win nor lose from them.

Nation, State, and Economy, pp. 39–40

The size of a state's territory therefore does not matter.

Nation, State, and Economy, p. 82

The right of self-determination in regard to the question of membership in a state thus means: whenever the inhabitants of a particular territory, whether it be a single village, a whole district, or a series of adjacent districts, make it known, by a freely conducted plebiscite, that they no longer wish to remain united to the state to which they belong at the time, but wish either to form an independent state or to attach themselves to some other state, their wishes are to be respected and complied with. This is the only feasible and effective way of preventing revolutions and civil and international wars.

Liberalism, p. 109

If it were in any way possible to grant this right of self-determination to every individual person, it would have to be done.

Liberalism, pp. 109–10

The situation of having to belong to a state to which one does not wish to belong is no less onerous if it is the result of an election than if one must endure it as the consequence of a military conquest.

Liberalism, p. 119

It makes no difference where the frontiers of a country are drawn. Nobody has a special material interest in enlarging the territory of the state in which he lives; nobody suffers loss if a part of this area is separated from the state. It is also immaterial whether all parts of the state's territory are in direct geographical connection, or whether they are separated by a piece of land belonging to another state. It is of no economic importance whether the country has a frontage on the ocean or not. In such a world the people of every village or district could decide by plebiscite to which state they wanted to belong.

Omnipotent Government, p. 92

SECURITY

There are in this world no such things as stability and security and no human endeavors are powerful enough to bring them about. There is in the social system of the market society no other means of acquiring wealth and of preserving it than successful service to the consumers.

Human Action, p. 227; p. 226

SELF-INTEREST

The member of a contractual society is free because he serves others only in serving himself. What restrains him is only the inevitable natural phenomenon of scarcity.

Human Action, p. 280; p. 283

With all the regard due to the sublime self-effacement of saints, we cannot help stating the fact that the world would be in a rather desolate condition if it were peopled exclusively by men not interested in the pursuit of material well-being.

Planning for Freedom, p. 146

Under such a socialist mode of production all personal incentives which selfishness provides under capitalism are removed, and a premium is put upon laziness and negligence. Whereas in a capitalist society selfishness incites everyone to the utmost diligence, in a socialist society it makes for inertia and laxity.

Human Action, p. 674; p. 677

Only those on the government's payroll are rated as unselfish and noble.

Human Action, No Entry; p. 735

In the society based on division of labour and co-operation, the interests of all members are in harmony, and it follows from this basic fact of social life that ultimately action in the interests of myself and action in the interest of others do not conflict, since the interests of individuals come together in the end.

Socialism, p. 357

That everyone lives and wishes to live primarily for himself does not disturb social life but promotes it, for the higher fulfillment of the individual's life is possible only in and through society.

Socialism, p. 361

In social cooperation everyone in serving his own interests serves the interests of his fellow men. Driven by the urge to improve his own conditions, he improves the conditions of other people. The baker does not hurt those for whom he bakes bread; he serves them.

The Ultimate Foundation of Economic Science, p. 88

SEX

If we do not wish to see life become extinct we should not call the source from which it is renewed a sink of vice.

Socialism, p. 88

Few men know how to be temperate in their sexual life, and it seems especially difficult for aging persons to understand that they should cease entirely to indulge in such pleasures or, at least, do so in moderation.

Liberalism, p. 53

SLAVERY

This is the difference between slavery and freedom. The slave must do what his superior orders him to do, but the free citizen—and this is what freedom means—is in a position to choose his own way of life.

Economic Policy, p. 23

Servile labor disappeared because it could not stand the competition of free labor; its unprofitability sealed its doom in the market economy.

Human Action, p. 625; p. 630

At no time and at no place was it possible for enterprises employing servile labor to compete on the market with enterprises employing free labor. Servile labor could always be utilized only where it did not have to meet the competition of free labor.

Human Action, p. 626; p. 630

When treated as a chattel, man renders a smaller yield per unit of cost expended for current sustenance and guarding than domestic animals.

Human Action, p. 626; pp. 630–31

Slavery did not prepare the way for division of labor. On the contrary it blocked the way. Indeed modern industrial society, with its highly developed division of labor, could not begin to grow until slavery had been abolished.

Socialism, p. 297

Private ownership in the means of production is the only necessary condition for the extensive development of the division of labor. The enslavement of the worker was not necessary to create it.

Socialism, p. 297

Everyone who preaches the right of the stronger considers himself as the stronger. He who espouses the institution of slavery never stops to reflect that he himself could be a slave.

Liberalism, p. 64

SMITH, ADAM

Smith did not inaugurate a new chapter in social philosophy and did not sow on land hitherto left uncultivated.

Economic Freedom and Interventionism, p. 115

Nobody should believe that he will find in Smith's *Wealth of Nations* information about present-day economics or about present-day problems of economic policy. Reading Smith is no more a substitute for studying economics than reading Euclid is a substitute for the study of mathematics.

Economic Freedom and Interventionism, p. 117

SOCIAL COOPERATION

What alone enables mankind to advance and distinguishes man from the animals is social cooperation.

Liberalism, p. 24

SOCIAL MOBILITY

To assign to everybody his proper place in society is the task of the consumers. Their buying and abstention from buying is instrumental in determining each individual's social position.

Human Action, p. 275; p. 275

Modern man has always before his eyes the possibility of growing rich by work and enterprise. In the more rigid economy of the past this was less easy. People were rich or poor from birth, and remained so through their lives unless they were given a change of position through some unforeseen accident, which their own work or enterprise could not have caused or avoided. Accordingly, we had the rich walking on the heights and the poor who stayed in the depths. It is not so in capitalistic society. The rich can more easily become poor and the poor can more easily become rich. And because every individual is not born with, as it were, his own or his family fate sealed, he tries to rise as high as he can.

Socialism, p. 395

SOCIAL PLANNING

The planner is a potential dictator who wants to deprive all other people of the power to plan and act according to their own plans. He aims at one thing only: the exclusive absolute preeminence of his own plan.

Planned Chaos, p. 29

It is a fact that men disagree in their value judgments. It is insolent to arrogate to oneself the right to overrule the plans of other people and to force them to submit to the plan of the planner.

Planned Chaos, p. 30

At the bottom of all this fanatical advocacy of planning and socialism there is often nothing else than the intimate consciousness of one's own inferiority and inefficiency.

Bureaucracy, p. 92

All this passionate praise of the supereminence of government action is but a poor disguise for the individual interventionist's self-deification. The great god State is a great god only because it is expected to do exclusively what the individual advocate of interventionism wants to see achieved.

Human Action, p. 727; pp. 731–32

The writings of the socialists are full of such utopian fancies. Whether they call themselves Marxian or non-Marxian socialists, technocrats, or simply planners, they are all eager to show how foolishly things are arranged in reality and how happily men could live if they were to invest the reformers with dictatorial powers. It is, they say, only the inadequacy of a capitalist mode of production that prevents mankind from enjoying all the amenities which could be produced under the contemporary state of technological knowledge.

Human Action, p. 503; pp. 506–07

The eyes with which we look at the matter must not be those of the dreamer envisioning a lost paradise, who sees the future in a blaze of rose-colored light, and condemns all that goes on around us.

Socialism, p. 92

If a man says socialism, or planning, he always has in view his own brand of socialism, his own plan. Thus planning does not in fact mean preparedness to cooperate peacefully. It means conflict.

Omnipotent Government, p. 243

The "social engineer" is the reformer who is prepared to "liquidate" all those who do not fit into his plan for the arrangement of human affairs.

The Ultimate Foundation of Economic Science, p. 94

SOCIAL SECURITY

Ultimately the granting of pensions amounts to a restriction of the wage earner's freedom to use his total income according to his own designs.

Planning for Freedom, p. 86

A man who is forced to provide of his own account for his old age must save a part of his income or take out an insurance policy. This leads him to examine the financial status of the savings bank or the insurance company or the soundness of the bonds he buys. Such a man is more likely to get an idea of the economic problems of his country than a man whom a pension scheme seemingly relieves of all worries.

Planning for Freedom, p. 92

It imposes upon the wage earners a restriction concerning the spending of their total income. It curtails the worker's freedom to arrange his household according to his own decisions. Whether such a system of social security is a good or a bad policy is essentially a political problem. One may try to justify it by declaring that the wage earners lack the insight and the moral strength to provide spontaneously for their own future. But then it is not easy to silence the voices of those who ask whether it is not paradoxical to entrust the nation's welfare to the decisions of voters whom the law itself considers incapable of managing their own affairs; whether it is not absurd to make those people supreme in the conduct of government who are manifestly in need of a guardian to prevent them from spending their own income foolishly.

Human Action, p. 613; p. 617

It is no accident that Germany, the country that inaugurated the social security system, was the cradle of both varieties of modern disparagement of democracy, the Marxian as well as the non-Marxian.

Human Action, p. 613; p. 617

By weakening or completely destroying the will to be well and able to work, social insurance creates illness and inability to work; it produces the habit of complaining—which is in itself a neurosis—and neuroses of other kinds. In short, it is an institution which tends to encourage disease, not to say accidents, and to intensify considerably the physical and psychic results of accidents and illnesses. As a social institution it makes a people sick bodily and mentally or at least helps to multiply, lengthen, and intensify disease.

Socialism, p. 432

SOCIALISM

There are many socialists who have never come to grips in any way with the problems of economics, and who have made no attempt at all to form for themselves any clear conception of the conditions which determine the character of human society.

Economic Calculation in the Socialist Commonwealth, p. 1

One may anticipate the nature of the future socialist society. There will be hundreds and thousands of factories in operation. Very few of these will be producing wares ready for use; in the majority of cases what will be manufactured will be unfinished goods and production goods. All these concerns will be inter-related. Every good will go through a whole series of stages before it is ready for use. In the ceaseless toil and moil of this process, however, the administration will be without any means of testing their bearings. It will never be able to determine whether a given good has not been kept for a superfluous length of time in the necessary processes of production, or whether work and material have not been wasted in its completion. How will it be able to decide whether this or that method of production is the more profitable? At best it will only be able to compare the quality and quantity of the consumable end product produced, but will in the rarest cases be in a position to compare the expenses entailed in production. It will know, or think it knows, the ends to be achieved by economic organization, and will have to regulate its activities accordingly, i.e. it will have to attain those ends with the least expense. It will have to make its computations with a view to finding the cheapest way. This computation will naturally have to be a value computation. It is eminently clear, and requires no further proof, that it cannot be of a technical character, and that it cannot be based upon the objective use value of goods and services.

Economic Calculation in the Socialist Commonwealth, pp. 22–23

In the socialist commonwealth every economic change becomes an undertaking whose success can be neither appraised in advance nor later retrospectively determined. There is only groping in the dark. Socialism is the abolition of rational economy.

Economic Calculation in the Socialist Commonwealth, p. 26

The Kingdom of Christ is not of this world; socialism, on the contrary, wants to establish the kingdom of salvation on earth. Therein lies its strength, therein, however, its weakness too, from which it will collapse some day just as quickly as it has triumphed.

Nation, State, and Economy, p. 208

229

Under socialism production is entirely directed by the orders of the central board of production management. The whole nation is an "industrial army" . . . and each citizen is bound to obey his superior's orders.

Planning for Freedom, p. 72

In the bureaucratic machine of socialism the way toward promotion is not achievement but the favor of the superiors.

Bureaucracy, p. 100

Socialism and democracy are irreconcilable.

A Critique of Interventionism, p. 79

The critics of the capitalistic order always seem to believe that the socialistic system of their dreams will do precisely what they think correct.

A Critique of Interventionism, pp. 156–57

A man who chooses between drinking a glass of milk and a glass of a solution of potassium cyanide does not choose between two beverages; he chooses between life and death. A society that chooses between capitalism and socialism does not choose between two social systems; it chooses between social cooperation and the disintegration of society. Socialism is not an alternative to capitalism; it is an alternative to any system under which men can live as *human beings*.

Human Action, p. 676; p. 680

Every socialist is a disguised dictator.

Human Action, p. 689; p. 693

People frequently call socialism a religion. It is indeed the religion of self-deification.

Human Action, p. 689; p. 693

Economics deals merely with the socialist plans, not with the psychological factors that impel people to espouse the religion of statolatry.

Human Action, p. 689; p. 693

Men must choose between the market economy and socialism. They cannot evade deciding between these alternatives by adopting a "middle-of-the-road" position, whatever name they may give to it.

Human Action, p. 857; p. 861

In abolishing economic calculation the general adoption of socialism would result in complete chaos and the disintegration of social cooperation under the division of labor.

Human Action, p. 857; p. 861

Socialism promises not only welfare—wealth for all—but universal happiness in love as well. This part of its program has been the source of much of its popularity.

Socialism, p. 74

Socialism is the renunciation of rational economy.

Socialism, p. 105

Everything brought forward in favor of Socialism during the last hundred years, in thousands of writings and speeches, all the blood which has been spilt by the supporters of Socialism, cannot make socialism workable.

Socialism, p. 117

The attempt to reform the world socialistically might destroy civilization. It would never set up a successful socialist community.

Socialism, p. 118

Socialist society is a society of officials. The way of living prevailing in it, and the mode of thinking of its members, are determined by this fact.

Socialism, p. 165

Socialism knows no freedom of choice in occupation. Everyone has to do what he is told to do and to go where he is sent.

Socialism, p. 165

Those who do not please the holders of power are not allowed to paint or to sculpt or to conduct an orchestra. Their works are not printed or performed.

Socialism, p. 166

The nationalization of intellectual life, which must be attempted under Socialism, must make all intellectual progress impossible.

Socialism, p. 167

No censor, no emperor, no pope, has ever possessed the power to suppress intellectual freedom which would be possessed by a socialist community.

Socialism, p. 169

That Socialism would be immediately practicable if an omnipotent and omniscient Deity were personally to descend to take in hand the government of human affairs is incontestable.

Socialism, p. 183

The ideas of modern Socialism have not sprung from proletarian brains. They were originated by intellectuals, sons of the bourgeoisie, not of wage-earners.

Socialism, p. 317

No one shall be idle if I have to work; no one shall be rich if I am poor. Thus we see, again and again, that resentment lies behind all socialist ideas.

Socialism, p. 394

The impracticability of Socialism is the result of intellectual, not moral, incapacity. . . . Even angels, if they were endowed only with human reason, could not form a socialistic community.

Socialism, p. 407

In fact Socialism is not in the least what it pretends to be. It is not the pioneer of a better and finer world, but the spoiler of what thousands of years of civilization have created. It does not build; it destroys. For destruction is the essence of it. It produces nothing, it only consumes what the social order based on private ownership in the means of production has created.

Socialism, p. 414

Not mythical "material productive forces," but reason and ideas determine the course of human affairs. What is needed to stop the trend toward socialism and despotism is common-sense and moral courage.

Planned Chaos, p. 90

Socialism is unrealizable as an economic system because a socialist society would not have any possibility of resorting to economic calculation. This is why it cannot be considered as a system of society's economic organization. It is a means to disintegrate social cooperation and to bring about poverty and chaos.

Money, Method, and the Market Process, p. 310

The socialists of Eastern Germany, the self-styled German Democratic Republic, spectacularly admitted the bankruptcy of the Marxian dreams when they built a wall to prevent their comrades from fleeing into the non-socialist part of Germany.

Money, Method, and the Market Process, p. 231

SOCIETY

It is always the individual who thinks. Society does not think any more than it eats or drinks. The evolution of human reasoning from the naive thinking of primitive man to the more subtle thinking of modern science took place within society. However, thinking itself is always an achievement of individuals. There is joint action, but no joint thinking.

Human Action, p. 177; p. 177

Society is essentially the mutual exchange of services.

Liberty and Property, pp. 18–19

Society is division of labor and combination of labor.

Human Action, p. 143; p. 143

We may call consciousness of kind, sense of community, or sense of belonging together the acknowledgement of the fact that all other human beings are potential collaborators in the struggle for survival because they are capable of recognizing the mutual benefits of cooperation.

Human Action, p. 144; p. 144

Society is division and association of labor. In the final analysis, there is no conflict of interest between society and the individual, as everyone can pursue his interest more efficiently in society than in isolation.

A Critique of Interventionism, p. 112

Civilization is an achievement of the "bourgeois" spirit, not of the spirit of conquest. Those barbarian peoples who did not substitute working for plundering disappeared from the historical scene.

Human Action, p. 645; p. 650

Society is the product of thought and will.

Socialism, p. 258

Man is inconceivable as an isolated being, for humanity exists only as a social phenomenon and mankind transcended the stage of animality only in so far as co-operation evolved the social relationships between the individuals. Evolution from the human animal to the human being was made possible by and achieved by means of social cooperation and by that alone.

Socialism, p. 259

Within the frame of social cooperation there can emerge between members of society feelings of sympathy and friendship and a sense of belonging together. These feelings are the source of man's most delightful and most sublime experiences. They are the most precious adornment of life; they lift the animal species man to the heights of a really human existence. However, they are not, as some have asserted, the agents that have brought about social relations. They are fruits of social cooperation.

Human Action, p. 144; p. 144

Human society is an intellectual and spiritual phenomenon. It is the outcome of a purposeful utilization of a universal law determining cosmic becoming, viz., the higher productivity of the division of labor. As with every instance of action, the recognition of the laws of nature is put into the service of man's efforts to improve his conditions.

Human Action, p. 145; p. 145

Every step by which an individual substitutes concerted action for isolated action results in an immediate and recognizable improvement in his conditions. The advantages derived from peaceful cooperation and division of labor are universal.

Human Action, p. 146; p. 146

SOUND MONEY

It is impossible to grasp the meaning of the idea of sound money if one does not realize that it was devised as an instrument for the protection of civil liberties against despotic inroads on the part of governments. Ideologically it belongs in the same class with political constitutions and bills of rights.

The Theory of Money and Credit, p. 454

Thus the sound-money principle has two aspects. It is affirmative in approving the market's choice of a commonly used medium of exchange. It is negative in obstructing the government's propensity to meddle with the currency system.

The Theory of Money and Credit, p. 455

There cannot be stable money within an environment dominated by ideologies hostile to the preservation of economic freedom.

The Theory of Money and Credit, p. 480

Sound money still means today what it meant in the nineteenth century: the gold standard.

The Theory of Money and Credit, p. 480

Perpetual vigilance on the part of the citizens can achieve what a thousand laws and dozens of alphabetical bureaus with hordes of employees never have and never will achieve: the preservation of a sound currency.

The Theory of Money and Credit, p. 495

SOVEREIGNTY

A state without territory is an empty concept. A state without sovereignty is a contradiction in terms.

Omnipotent Government, p. 46

SPECULATION

Without speculation there can be no economic activity reaching beyond the immediate present.

Socialism, p. 125

Speculation is the link that binds isolated economic action to the economic activity of society as a whole.

Socialism, p. 182

Speculation in the capitalist system performs a function which must be performed in any economic system however organized: it provides for the adjustment of supply and demand over time and space.

Socialism, p. 125

Speculation performs an economic service which cannot conceivably be eliminated from any economic system.

Socialism, p. 125

Every action is a speculation, i.e., guided by a definite opinion concerning the uncertain conditions of the future.

The Ultimate Foundation of Economic Science, p. 51

The influence of speculation cannot alter the average level of prices over a given period; what it can do is to diminish the gap between the highest and the lowest prices. Price fluctuations are reduced by speculation, not aggravated, as the popular legend has it.

The Theory of Money and Credit, p. 286

Speculation anticipates future price changes; its economic function consists in evening out price differences between different places and different points in time and, through the pressure which prices exert on production and consumption, in adapting stocks and demands to each other.

Nation, State, and Economy, p. 145

SPIRIT

Not with weapons but only with the spirit can a minority overcome the majority.

Nation, State, and Economy, p. 106

What warrants success in a fight for freedom and civilization is not merely material equipment but first of all the spirit that animates those handling the weapons. This heroic spirit cannot be bought by inflation.

The Theory of Money and Credit, p. 469

SPORTS

Games are not reality, but merely play. They are civilized man's outlet for deeply ingrained instincts of enmity. When the game comes to an end, the victors and the defeated shake hands and return to the reality of their social life, which is cooperation and not fighting.

The Ultimate Foundation of Economic Science, p. 88

A game is a pastime, is a means to employ one's leisure time and to banish boredom.

The Ultimate Foundation of Economic Science, p. 90

No game can, apart from the pleasure it gives to the players and to the spectators, contribute anything to the improvement of human conditions.

The Ultimate Foundation of Economic Science, p. 90

STANDARD OF LIVING

The characteristic feature of modern capitalism is mass production of goods destined for consumption by the masses. The result is a tendency towards a continuous improvement in the average standard of living, a progressing enrichment of the many.

The Anti-Capitalistic Mentality, p. 1

Under capitalism the common man enjoys amenities which in ages gone by were unknown and therefore inaccessible even to the richest people.

The Anti-Capitalistic Mentality, p. 3

The European worker today lives under more favorable and more agreeable outward circumstances than the pharaoh of Egypt once did, in spite of the fact that the pharaoh commanded thousands of slaves, while the worker has nothing to depend on but the strength and skill of his hands.

Liberalism, pp. 22–23

The standard of living of the common man is highest in those countries which have the greatest number of wealthy entrepreneurs.

Planning for Freedom, p. 135

How uneasy an American worker would be if he were forced to live in the style of a medieval lord and to miss the plumbing facilities and the other gadgets he simply takes for granted!

Human Action, pp. 612; p. 616

Mankind has not reached the stage of ultimate technological perfection. There is ample room for further progress and for further improvement of the standards of living. The creative and inventive spirit subsists notwithstanding all assertions to the contrary. But it flourishes only where there is economic freedom.

Omnipotent Government, p. x

STATE

The ordered organization of coercion we call the State.

Socialism, p. 280

The essential feature of government is the enforcement of its decrees by beating, killing, and imprisoning. Those who are asking for more government interference are asking ultimately for more compulsion and less freedom.

Human Action, p. 715; p. 719

The whole of mankind's progress has had to be achieved against the resistance and opposition of the state and its power of coercion.

Liberalism, p. 58

A new type of superstition has got hold of people's minds, the worship of the state. People demand the exercise of the methods of coercion and compulsion, of violence and threat. Woe to anybody who does not bend his knee to the fashionable idols!

Omnipotent Government, p. 11

The worship of the state is the worship of force. There is no more dangerous menace to civilization than a government of incompetent, corrupt, or vile men. The worst evils which mankind ever had to endure were inflicted by bad governments. The state can be and has often been in the course of history the main source of mischief and disaster.

Omnipotent Government, p. 47

He who proclaims the godliness of the State and the infallibility of its priests, the bureaucrats, is considered as an impartial student of the social sciences.

Planned Chaos, p. 16

It is characteristic of current political thinking to welcome every suggestion which aims at enlarging the influence of government.

On the Manipulation of Money and Credit, p. 107

How fine the world would be if the "State" were free to cure all ills! It is one step only from such a mentality to the perfect totalitarianism of Stalin and Hitler.

Bureaucracy, pp. 75–76

No reform can render perfectly satisfactory the operation of an institution the essential activity of which consists in inflicting pain.

The Ultimate Foundation of Economic Science, p. 100

Every step a government takes beyond the fulfillment of its essential functions of protecting the smooth operation of the market economy against aggression, whether on the part of domestic or foreign disturbers, is a step forward on the road that directly leads into the totalitarian system where there is no freedom at all.

Human Action, No Entry; p. 282

Louis XIV was very frank and sincere when he said: I am the State. The modern etatist is modest. He says: I am the servant of the State; but, he implies, the State is God. You could revolt against a Bourbon king, and the French did it. This was, of course, a struggle of man against man. But you cannot revolt against the god State and against his humble handy man, the bureaucrat.

Bureaucracy, pp. 74–75

Après nous le déluge (After us, the deluge) is an old maxim of government.

Socialism, p. 179

There is no reason to idolize the police power and ascribe to its omnipotence and omniscience. There are things which it can certainly not accomplish. It cannot conjure away the scarcity of the factors of production, it cannot make people more prosperous, it cannot raise the productivity of labor. All it can achieve is to prevent gangsters from frustrating the efforts of those people who are intent upon promoting material well-being.

Human Action, p. 827; p. 831

It is not God. It is simply compulsion and coercion; it is the police power.

Omnipotent Government, p. 47

The state is a human institution, not a superhuman being. He who says "state" means coercion and compulsion. He who says: There should be a law concerning this matter, means: The armed men of the government should force people to do what they do not want to do, or not to do what they like. He who says: This law should be better enforced, means: the police should force people to obey this law. He who says: The state is God, deifies arms and prisons.

Omnipotent Government, p. 47

Not every apparatus of compulsion and coercion is called a state. Only one which is powerful enough to maintain its existence, for some time at least, by its own force is commonly called a state. A gang of robbers, which because of the comparative weakness of its forces has no prospect of successfully resisting for any length of time the forces of another organization, is not entitled to be called a state. The state will either smash or tolerate a gang. In the first case the gang is not a state because its independence lasts for a short time only; in the second case it is not a state because it does not stand on its own might.

Omnipotent Government, p. 46

The apparatus of compulsion and coercion is always operated by mortal men.

Omnipotent Government, p. 47

We see that as soon as we surrender the principle that the state should not interfere in any questions touching of the individual's mode of life, we end by regulating and restricting the latter down to the smallest detail. The personal freedom of the individual is abrogated. He becomes a slave of the community bound to obey the dictates of the majority.

Liberalism, p. 54

The essence of etatism is to take from one group in order to give to another. The more it can take the more it can give. It is to the interest of those whom the government wishes to favor that their state become as large as possible.

Omnipotent Government, p. 94

Whoever wishes peace among peoples must fight statism.

Nation, State, and Economy, p. 77

STATISTICS

Statistics is a method for the presentation of historical facts concerning prices and other relevant data of human action. It is not economics and cannot produce economic theorems and theories. The statistics of prices is economic history.

Human Action, p. 348; p. 351

There is no such thing as quantitative economics.

Human Action, p. 348; p. 351

Figures alone prove or disprove nothing. Only the conclusions drawn from the collected material can do this. And these are theoretical.

Socialism, p. 325

The idea that changes in the purchasing power of money may be measured is scientifically untenable.

On the Manipulation of Money and Credit, p. 88

It is not possible even to *measure* variations in the purchasing power of money.

The Theory of Money and Credit, p. 257

Statistics is the description in numerical terms of experiences concerning phenomena not subject to regular uniformity. . . . Statistics is therefore a specific method of history.

The Ultimate Foundation of Economic Science, p. 55

There is an inclination in the United States and in Anglo-Saxon countries generally to overestimate in a quite extraordinary manner the significance of index methods. In these countries, it is entirely overlooked that the scientific exactness of these methods leaves much to be desired, that they can never yield anything more than a rough result at best, and that the question whether one or other method of calculation is preferable can never be solved by scientific means.

The Theory of Money and Credit, pp. 445–46

SYNDICALISM

The syndicalistically organized state would be no socialist state but a state of worker capitalism, since the individual worker groups would be owners of the capital. Syndicalism would make all repatterning of production impossible; it leaves no room free for economic progress. In its entire intellectual character it suits the age of peasants and craftsmen, in which economic relations are rather stationary.

Nation, State, and Economy, p. 199

It is not unfair to call syndicalism the economic philosophy of short-sighted people, of those adamant conservatives who look askance upon any innovation and are so blinded by envy that they call down curses upon those who provide them with more, better, and cheaper products. They are like patients who grudge the doctor his success in curing them of a malady.

Human Action, p. 810; p. 814

TARIFFS

All that a tariff can achieve is to divert production from those locations in which the output per unit of input is higher to locations in which it is lower. It does not increase production; it curtails it.

Human Action, p. 737; p. 744

The only case that can be made on behalf of protective tariffs is this: the sacrifices they impose could be offset by other, noneconomic advantages—for instance, from a national and military point of view it could be desirable to more or less isolate a country from the world.

A Critique of Interventionism, p. 23

The imposition of a duty on the importation of a commodity burdens the consumers.

Human Action, p. 742; p. 749

Many people look upon tariff protection as if it were a privilege accorded to their nation's wage earners, procuring them, for the full duration of its existence, a higher standard of living than they would enjoy under free trade.

Human Action, p. 745; p. 752

TAXES

Some experts have declared that it is necessary to tax the people until it hurts. I disagree with these sadists.

Defense, Controls, and Inflation, p. 333

If the present tax rates had been in effect from the beginning of our century, many who are millionaires today would live under more modest circumstances. But all those new branches of industry which supply the masses with articles unheard of before would operate, if at all, on a much smaller scale, and their products would be beyond the reach of the common man.

Planning for Freedom, p. 16

Taxing profits is tantamount to taxing success.

Planning for Freedom, p. 121

Estate taxes of the height they have already attained for the upper brackets are no longer to be qualified as taxes. They are measures of expropriation.

Planning for Freedom, p. 32

Progressive taxation of income and profits means that precisely those parts of the income which people would have saved and invested are taxed away.

Economic Policy, p. 84

The metamorphosis of taxes into weapons of destruction is the mark of present-day public finance.

Human Action, p. 734; p. 741

Taxes are paid because the taxpayers are afraid of offering resistance to the tax gatherers. They know that any disobedience or resistance is hopeless. As long as this is the state of affairs, the government is able to collect the money that it wants to spend.

Human Action, No Entry; p. 719

Taxes are necessary. But the system of discriminatory taxation universally accepted under the misleading name of progressive taxation of income and inheritance is not a mode of taxation. It is rather a mode of disguised expropriation of the successful capitalists and entrepreneurs.

Human Action, p. 803; p. 807

Nothing is more calculated to make a demagogue popular than a constantly reiterated demand for heavy taxes on the rich. Capital levies and high income taxes on the larger incomes are extraordinarily popular with the masses, who do not have to pay them.

Socialism, p. 447

TECHNOLOGY

What begot all those technological and therapeutical achievements that characterize our age was not science, but the social and political system of capitalism. Only in the climate of huge capital accumulation could experimentalism develop from a pastime of geniuses like Archimedes and Leonardo da Vinci into a well-organized systematic pursuit of knowledge.

The Ultimate Foundation of Economic Science, p. 127

The research activities of the experimental natural sciences are in themselves neutral with regard to any philosophical and political issue. But they can thrive and become beneficial for mankind only where there prevails a social philosophy of individualism and freedom.

The Ultimate Foundation of Economic Science, p. 128

THEORY

There cannot be too much of a correct theory.

Epistemological Problems of Economics, p. 141

TIME

Man is subject to the passing of time. He comes into existence, grows, becomes old, and passes away. His time is scarce. He must economize it as he economizes other scarce factors.

Human Action, p. 101; p. 101

Time for man is not a homogenous substance of which only length counts. It is not a *more* or a *less* in dimension. . . . It is an irreversible flux the fractions of which appear in different perspective according to whether they are nearer to or remoter from the instant of valuation and decision. Satisfaction of a want in the nearer future is, other things being equal, preferred to that in the farther distant future. Present goods are more valuable than future goods.

Human Action, pp. 480–81; p. 483

The value of time, i.e., time preference or the higher valuation of want-satisfaction in nearer periods of the future as against that in remoter periods, is an essential element in human action. It determines every choice and every action.

There is no man for whom the difference between sooner and later does not count. The time element is instrumental in the formation of all prices of all commodities and services.

Human Action, p. 490; p. 493

TOLERANCE

A free man must be able to endure it when his fellow men act and live otherwise than he considers proper. He must free himself from the habit, just as soon as something does not please him, of calling for the police.

Liberalism, p. 55

TOTALITARIANISM

It is vain to fight totalitarianism by adopting totalitarian methods. Freedom can only be won by men unconditionally committed to the principles of freedom. The first requisite for a better social order is the return to unrestricted freedom of thought and speech.

Omnipotent Government, p. 14

TREATY OF VERSAILLES

The four peace treaties of Versailles, Saint Germain, Trianon, and Sèvres together form the most clumsy diplomatic settlement ever carried out. They will be remembered as outstanding examples of political failure.

Omnipotent Government, p. 211

The Treaty of Versailles was not unfair to Germany and it did not plunge the German people into misery.

Omnipotent Government, p. 211

It is a grotesque misrepresentation of the facts to assert that these payments made Germany poor and condemned the Germans to starvation. They would not have seriously affected the German standard of living even if the Germans had paid these sums out of their own pockets and not, as they did in fact, out of money borrowed from abroad.

Omnipotent Government, p. 214

TRUTH

Truth has its own way. It works and produces effects even if party programs and textbooks refuse to acknowledge it as truth.

Planning for Freedom, p. 11

Truth is not the halfway point between two untruths.

On the Manipulation of Money and Credit, p. 88

Yet the criterion of truth is that it works even if nobody is prepared to acknowledge it.

The Ultimate Foundation of Economic Science, p. 94

At least one of the characteristic marks of a true theory is that action based on it succeeds in attaining the expected result. In this sense, truth works while untruth does not work.

Theory and History, p. 123

Truth persists and works, even if nobody is left to utter it.

Austrian Economics: An Anthology, p. 76

Truth refers to what is or was, not to a state of affairs that is not or was not but would suit the wishes of the truth-seeker better.

Theory and History, p. 298

Governments, political parties, pressure groups, and the bureaucrats of the educational hierarchy think they can avoid the inevitable consequences of unsuitable measures by boycotting and silencing the independent economists. But truth persists and works, even if nobody is left to utter it.

The Historical Setting of the Austrian School, p. 45

TYRANNY

In the hegemonic state there is neither right nor law; there are only directives and regulations which the director may change daily and apply with what discrimination he pleases which the wards must obey. The wards have one freedom only: to obey without asking questions.

Human Action, p. 199; p. 198

The substitution of economic planning for the market economy removes all freedom and leaves to the individual merely the right to obey. The authority directing all economic matters controls all aspects of a man's life and activities. It is the only employer. All labor becomes compulsory labor because the employee must accept what the chief deigns to offer him. The economic tsar determines what and how much of each the consumer may consume. There is no sector of human life in which a decision is left to the individual's value judgments. The authority assigns a definite task to him, trains him for his job, and employs him at the place and in the manner it deems expedient.

Human Action, p. 284; p. 287

A man is free as far as he shapes his life according to his own plans. A man whose fate is determined by the plans of a superior authority, in which the exclusive power to plan is vested, is not free in the sense in which the term "free" was used and understood by all people until the semantic revolution of our day brought about a confusion of tongues.

Human Action, p. 285; p. 287

It is the subordination of every individual's whole life, work, and leisure, to the orders of those in power and office. It is the reduction of man to a cog in an all-embracing machine of compulsion and coercion. It forces the individual to renounce any activity of which the government does not approve. It tolerates no expression of dissent. It is the transformation of society into a strictly disciplined labor-army.

Bureaucracy, p. 17

It holds the individual in tight rein from the womb to the tomb.

Bureaucracy, p. 17

UNCERTAINTY

The most that can be attained with regard to reality is probability.

Human Action, p. 105; p. 105

The uncertainty of the future is already implied in the very notion of action. That man acts and that the future is uncertain are by no means two independent matters. They are only two different modes of establishing one thing.

Human Action, p. 105; p. 105

Understanding is always based on incomplete knowledge.

Human Action, p. 112; p. 112

There is in the course of human events no stability and consequently no safety.

Human Action, p. 113; p. 113

In the universe there is never and nowhere stability and immobility. Change and transformation are essential features of life. Each state of affairs is transient; each age is an age of transition. In human life there is never calm and repose. Life is a process, not a perseverance in a *status quo*.

The Anti-Capitalistic Mentality, p. 106

It is certainly true that the necessity of adjusting oneself again and again to changing conditions is onerous. But change is the essence of life. In an unhampered market economy the absence of security, i.e., the absence of protection for vested interests, is the principle that makes for a steady improvement in material well-being.

Human Action, p. 848; p. 852

It is a poor makeshift to call any age an age of transition. In the living world there is always change. Every age is an age of transition.

Human Action, p. 855; p. 860

One of the fundamental conditions of man's existence and action is the fact that he does not know what will happen in the future.

Theory and History, p. 180

What a man can say about the future is always merely speculative anticipation.

Theory and History, p. 203

UNEMPLOYMENT

Government spending cannot create additional jobs. If the government provides the funds required by taxing the citizens or by borrowing from the public, it abolishes on the one hand as many jobs as it creates on the other.

Planned Chaos, pp. 20–21

It is obviously futile to attempt to eliminate unemployment by embarking upon a program of public works that would otherwise not have been undertaken. The necessary resources for such projects must be withdrawn by taxes or loans from the application they would otherwise have found. Unemployment in one industry can, in this way, be mitigated only to the extent that it is increased in another.

Liberalism, p. 85

Labor is more scarce than material factors of production.

Human Action, p. 136; p. 136

If a job-seeker cannot obtain the position he prefers, he must look for another kind of job. If he cannot find an employer ready to pay him as much as he would like to earn, he must abate his pretensions. If he refuses, he will not get any job. He remains unemployed. What causes unemployment is the fact that—contrary to the above-mentioned doctrine of the worker's inability to wait—those eager to earn wages can and do wait.

Human Action, p. 595; p. 598

Mass unemployment is not proof of the failure of capitalism, but the proof of the failure of traditional union methods.

Planning for Freedom, p. 13

On a free labor market wage rates tend toward a height at which all employers ready to pay these rates can find all the men they need and all the workers ready to work for this rate can find jobs. There prevails a tendency toward full employment.

Planning for Freedom, p. 84

There prevails on a free labor market a tendency toward full employment.

Planning for Freedom, p. 153

The result of the governments' and the unions' meddling with the height of wage rates cannot be anything else than an incessant increase in the number of unemployed.

Planning for Freedom, p. 192

Permanent mass unemployment destroys the moral foundations of the social order. The young people, who, having finished their training for work, are forced to remain idle, are the ferment out of which the most radical political movements are formed. In their ranks the soldiers of the coming revolutions are recruited.

Socialism, p. 440

The need of society for labor is never satisfied.

Socialism, p. 129

Unemployment is a problem of wages, not of work.

Socialism, p. 439

It is not capitalism which is responsible for the evils of permanent mass unemployment, but the policy which paralyses its working.

Socialism, p. 441

There is but one remedy for lasting unemployment of great masses; the abandonment of the policy of raising wage rates by government decree or by the application or the threat of violence.

Omnipotent Government, p. 65

UNEMPLOYMENT INSURANCE

Unemployment doles can have no other effect than the perpetuation of unemployment.

Socialism, p. 440

Assistance granted to the unemployed does not dispose of unemployment. It makes it easier for the unemployed to remain idle.

Human Action, p. 770; p. 776

For the unemployed to be granted support by the government or by the unions only serves to enlarge the evil. If what is involved is a case of unemployment springing from dynamic changes in the economy, then the unemployment benefits only result in postponing the adjustment of the workers to the new conditions.

Liberalism, p. 84

UNIONS

Exclusively preoccupied with wage rates and pensions, the unions boast of their Pyrrhic victories. The union members are not conscious of the fact that their fate is tied up with the flowering of their employers' enterprises.

Planning for Freedom, p. 91

The labor unions are deadly foes of every new machine.

Human Action, p. 269; p. 269

They and their members and officials have acquired the power and the right to commit wrongs to person and property, to deprive individuals of the means of earning a livelihood, and to commit many other acts which no one can do with impunity.

Planning for Freedom, p. 191

As people think that they owe to unionism their high standard of living, they condone violence, coercion, and intimidation on the part of unionized labor and are indifferent to the curtailment of personal freedom inherent in the union-shop and closed-shop clauses.

Planning for Freedom, p. 153

The labor unions aim at a monopolistic position on the labor market. But once they have attained it, their policies are restrictive and not monopoly price policies. They are intent upon restricting the supply of labor in their field without bothering about the fate of those excluded.

Human Action, p. 374; p. 377

No social cooperation under the division of labor is possible when some people or unions of people are granted the right to prevent by violence and the threat of violence other people from working.

Planned Chaos, p. 27

The labor unions of the Anglo-Saxon countries favored participation in the Great War in order to eliminate the last remnants of the liberal doctrine of free movement and migration of labor.

A Critique of Interventionism, p. 123

No one has ever succeeded in the effort to demonstrate that unionism could improve the conditions and raise the standard of living of *all* those eager to earn wages.

Human Action, pp. 764–65; pp. 770–71

The issue is not the right to form associations. It is whether or not any association of private citizens should be granted the privilege of resorting with impunity to violent action. It is the same problem that relates to the activities of the Ku Klux Klan.

Human Action, p. 773; p. 779

Strikes, sabotage, violent action and terrorism of every kind are not economic means. They are destructive means, designed to interrupt the movement of economic life. They are weapons of war which must inevitably lead to the destruction of society.

Socialism, p. 307

The cornerstone of trade unionism is compulsory membership.

Socialism, p. 435

The weapon of the trade union is the strike. It must be borne in mind that every strike is an act of coercion, a form of extortion, a measure of violence directed against all who might act in opposition to the strikers' intentions.

Socialism, p. 435

The policy of strike, violence, and sabotage can claim no merit whatever for any improvement in the workers' position.

Socialism, p. 437

UNITED NATIONS

The United Nations is simply a meeting place for useless discussions.

Economic Policy, p. 85

The League of Nations did not fail because its organization was deficient. It failed because it lacked the spirit of genuine liberalism. It was a convention of governments imbued with the spirit of economic nationalism and entirely committed to the principles of economic warfare.

Human Action, p. 683; pp. 687–88

It is futile to place confidence in treaties, conferences, and such bureaucratic outfits as the League of Nations and the United Nations. Plenipotentiaries, office clerks and experts make a poor show in fighting ideologies. The spirit of conquest cannot be smothered by red tape. What is needed is a radical change in ideologies and economic policies.

Human Action, p. 821; p. 825

UTOPIANS

The characteristic feature of all utopian plans from that of Plato down to that of Marx is the rigid petrification of all human conditions. Once the "perfect" state of social affairs is attained, no further changes ought to be tolerated.

The Ultimate Foundation of Economic Science, p. 123

VALUE

Value is not intrinsic, it is not in things. It is within us; it is the way in which man reacts to the conditions of his environment. Neither is value in words and doctrines, it is reflected in human conduct. It is not what a man or groups of men say about value that counts, but how they act.

Human Action, p. 96; p. 96

A judgment of value does not measure, it arranges in a scale of degrees, it grades. It is expressive of an order of preference and sequence, but not expressive of measure and weight.

Human Action, p. 97; p. 97

It is vain to speak of any calculation of values. Calculation is possible only with cardinal numbers. The difference between the valuation of two states of affairs is entirely psychical and personal. It is not open to any projection into the external world. It can be sensed only by the individual. It cannot be communicated or imparted to any fellow man.

Human Action, p. 97; p. 97

There is no yardstick to measure the aesthetic worth of a poem or of a building.

The Anti-Capitalistic Mentality, p. 75

There is no method available to construct a unit of value.

Human Action, p. 206; p. 205

Value is not intrinsic. It is not in things and conditions but in the valuing subject.

Theory and History, p. 23

There are no such things as absolute values, independent of the subjective preferences of erring men. Judgments of values are the outcome of human arbitrariness. They reflect all the shortcomings and weaknesses of their authors.

Bureaucracy, p. 26

WAGE RATES

Like other factors of production, labor is also valued according to its usefulness in satisfying human wants.

On the Manipulation of Money and Credit, p. 177

In the long run the worker can never get more than the consumer allows.

Bureaucracy, p. 37

There is but one way toward an increase of real wage rates for all those eager to earn wages: the progressive accumulation of new capital and the improvement of technical methods of production which the new capital brings about. The true interests of labor coincide with those of business.

Bureaucracy, p. 112

The only means to raise wage rates permanently for all those eager to earn wages is to raise the productivity of labor by increasing the per-head quota of capital invested and improving the methods of production.

Planning for Freedom, p. 6

The buyers do not pay for the toil and trouble the worker took nor for the length of time he spent in working. They pay for the products.

Planning for Freedom, p. 151

The better the tools are which the worker uses in his job, the more he can perform in an hour, the higher is, consequently, his remuneration.

Planning for Freedom, p. 151

The height of wage rates is determined by the consumers' appraisal of the value the worker's labor adds to the value of the article available for sale.

Planning for Freedom, p. 190

It is *not* the Hollywood film corporation that pays the wages of a movie star; it is the people who pay admission to the movies. And it is *not* the entrepreneurs of a boxing match who pay the enormous demands of the prize fighters; it is the people who pay admission to the fight.

Economic Policy, p. 9–10

There is only one efficacious way toward a rise in real wage rates and an improvement of the standard of living of the wage earners: to increase the per-head quota of capital invested.

The Theory of Money and Credit, p. 464–65

Minimum wage rates, whether decreed and enforced by the government or by labor union pressure and violence, result in mass unemployment.

Planning for Freedom, p. 27

WAR AND PEACE

Whoever wishes peace among peoples must fight statism.

Nation, State, and Economy, p. 77

Modern society, based as it is on the division of labor, can be preserved only under conditions of lasting peace.

Liberalism, p. 44

The market economy involves peaceful cooperation. It bursts asunder when the citizens turn into warriors and, instead of exchanging commodities and services, fight one another.

Human Action, p. 817; p. 821

Modern war is not a war of royal armies. It is a war of the peoples, a total war. It is a war of states which do not leave to their subjects any private sphere; they consider the whole population a part of the armed forces. Whoever does not fight must work for the support and equipment of the army. Army and people are one and the same. The citizens passionately participate in the war. For it is their state, their God, who fights.

Omnipotent Government, p. 104

What the incompatibility of war and capitalism really means is that war and high civilization are incompatible.

Human Action, p. 824; p. 828

Society has arisen out of the works of peace; the essence of society is peacemaking. Peace and not war is the father of all things. Only economic action has created the wealth around us; labor, not the profession of arms, brings happiness. Peace builds, war destroys.

Socialism, p. 59

All the materials needed for the conduct of a war must be provided by restriction of civilian consumption, by using up a part of the capital available and by working harder. The whole burden of warring falls upon the living generation.

Human Action, p. 228; p. 227

At the breakfast table of every citizen sits in wartime an invisible guest, as it were, a G.I. who shares the meal. In the citizen's garage stays not only the family car but besides—invisibly—a tank or a plane. The important fact is that this G.I. needs more in food, clothing, and other things than he used to consume as a civilian and that military equipment wears out much quicker than civilian equipment. The costs of a modern war are enormous.

Defense, Controls, and Inflation, p. 331

Men are fighting one another because they are convinced that the extermination and liquidation of adversaries is the only means of promoting their own well-being.

Human Action, p. 175; p. 176

The existence of the armaments industries is a consequence of the warlike spirit, not its cause.

Human Action, p. 297; p. 300

What basis for war could there still be, once all peoples had been set free?

Nation, State, and Economy, p. 35

The liberal thinks otherwise. He is convinced that victorious war is an evil even for the victor, that peace is always better than war. He demands no sacrifice from the stronger, but only that he should come to realize where his true interests lie and learn to understand that peace is for him, the stronger, just as advantageous as it is for the weaker.

Liberalism, p. 24

Wars, foreign and domestic (revolutions, civil wars), are more likely to be avoided the closer the division of labor binds men.

A Critique of Interventionism, p. 115

The pacifistic line of argument goes too far if it simply denies that a people can gain by war.

Nation, State, and Economy, pp. 152–53

War is the alternative to freedom of foreign investment as realized by the international capital market.

Human Action, p. 499; p. 502

The statement that one man's boon is the other man's damage is valid with regard to robbery, war, and booty. The robber's plunder is the damage of the despoiled victim. But war and commerce are two different things.

Human Action, p. 662; p. 666

The philosophy of protectionism is a philosophy of war. The wars of our age are not at variance with popular economic doctrines; they are, on the contrary, the inescapable result of consistent application of these doctrines.

Human Action, p. 683; p. 687

What has transformed the limited war between royal armies into total war, the clash between peoples, is not technicalities of military art, but the substitution of the welfare state for the laissez-faire state.

Human Action, p. 820; p. 824

Under laissez faire peaceful coexistence of a multitude of sovereign nations is possible. Under government control of business it is impossible.

Human Action, p. 820; p. 824

In the long run war and the preservation of the market economy are incompatible. Capitalism is essentially a scheme for peaceful nations. But this does not mean that a nation which is forced to repel foreign aggressors must substitute government control for private enterprise. If it were to do this, it would deprive itself of the most efficient means of defense. There is no record of a socialist nation which defeated a capitalist nation. In spite of their much glorified war socialism, the Germans were defeated in both World Wars.

Human Action, p. 824; p. 828

The emergence of the international division of labor requires the total abolition of war.

Human Action, p. 827; p. 831

Modern war is merciless, it does not spare pregnant women or infants; it is indiscriminate killing and destroying. It does not respect the rights of neutrals. Millions are killed, enslaved, or expelled from the dwelling places in which their ancestors lived for centuries. Nobody can foretell what will happen in the next chapter of this endless struggle. This has little to do with the atomic bomb. The root of the evil is not the construction of new, more dreadful weapons. It is the spirit of conquest. It is probable that scientists will discover some methods of defense against the atomic bomb. But this will not alter things, it will merely prolong for a short time the process of the complete destruction of civilization.

Human Action, p. 828; p. 832

To defeat the aggressors is not enough to make peace durable. The main thing is to discard the ideology that generates war.

Human Action, p. 828; p. 832

Ownership turns the fighting man into the economic man. Only the exclusion of private property can maintain the military character of the State. Only the warrior, who has no other occupation apart from war than preparation for war, is always ready for war. Men occupied in affairs may wage wars of defense but not long wars of conquest.

Socialism, pp. 220–21

Within a world of free trade and democracy there are no incentives for war and conquest.

Omnipotent Government, p. 3

Only in the case of primitive peoples does war lead to the selection of the stronger and more gifted, and that among civilized peoples it leads to a deterioration of the race by unfavorable selection.

Socialism, p. 290

The only means to lasting peace is to remove the root causes of war.

Omnipotent Government, p. 6

But what is needed for a satisfactory solution of the burning problem of international relations is neither a new office with more committees, secretaries, commissioners, reports, and regulations, nor a new body of armed executioners, but the radical overthrow of mentalities and domestic policies which must result in conflict.

Omnipotent Government, p. 6

Full freedom of movement of persons and goods, the most comprehensive protection of the property and freedom of each individual, removal of all state compulsion in the school system, in short, the most exact and complete application of the ideas of 1789, are the prerequisites of peaceful conditions.

Nation, State, and Economy, p. 96

If you want to abolish war, you must eliminate its causes. What is needed is to restrict government activities to the preservation of life, health, and private property, and thereby to safeguard the working of the market. Sovereignty must not be used for inflicting harm on anyone, whether citizen or foreigner.

Omnipotent Government, p. 138

If some peoples pretend that history or geography gives them the right to subjugate other races, nations, or peoples, there can be no peace.

Omnipotent Government, p. 15

Only one thing can conquer war—that liberal attitude of mind which can see nothing in war but destruction and annihilation, and which can never wish to bring about a war, because it regards war as injurious even to the victors.

The Theory of Money and Credit, p. 433

If war is regarded as advantageous, then laws . . . will not be allowed to stand in the way of going to war. On the first day of any war, all the laws opposing obstacles to it will be swept aside.

The Theory of Money and Credit, p. 434

269

The way to eternal peace does not lead through strengthening state and central power, as socialism strives for.

Nation, State, and Economy, p. 96

History has witnessed the failure of many endeavors to impose peace by war, cooperation by coercion, unanimity by slaughtering dissidents. . . . A lasting order cannot be established by bayonets.

Omnipotent Government, pp. 6–7

War can really cause no economic boom, at least not directly, since an increase in wealth never does result from destruction of goods.

Nation, State, and Economy, p. 154

Not through war and victory but only through work can a nation create the preconditions for the well-being of its members. Conquering nations finally perish, either because they are annihilated by strong ones or because the ruling class is culturally overwhelmed by the subjugated.

Nation, State, and Economy, p. 87

Economically considered, war and revolution are always bad business.

Nation, State, and Economy, p. 152

The essence of so-called war prosperity; it enriches some by what it takes from others. It is not rising wealth but a shifting of wealth and income.

Nation, State, and Economy, p. 158

There is but one field of public administration in which the criterion of success or failure is unquestionable: the waging of war. But even here the only thing certain is whether the operation has been crowned with success.

Liberalism, p. 98

War socialism was by no means complete socialism, but it was full and true socialization without exception if one had kept on the path that had been taken.

Nation, State, and Economy, p. 173

War prosperity is like the prosperity that an earthquake or a plague brings. The earthquake means good business for construction workers, and cholera improves the business of physicians, pharmacists, and undertakers; but no one has for that reason yet sought to celebrate earthquakes and cholera as stimulators of the productive forces in the general interest.

Nation, State, and Economy, p. 154

Interventionism generates economic nationalism, and economic nationalism generates bellicosity. If men and commodities are prevented from crossing the borderlines, why should not the armies try to pave the way for them?

Human Action, p. 828; p. 832

WEALTH

The riches of successful entrepreneurs is not the cause of anybody's poverty; it is the consequence of the fact that the consumers are better supplied than they would have been in the absence of the entrepreneur's effort.

Planning for Freedom, p. 135

A wealthy man can preserve his wealth only by continuing to serve the consumers in the most efficient way.

Human Action, p. 272; p. 271

No investment is safe forever. He who does not use his property in serving the consumers in the most efficient way is doomed to failure.

Human Action, p. 308; p. 312

Profit is not related to or dependent on the amount of capital employed by the entrepreneur. Capital does not "beget" profit. Profit and loss are entirely determined by the success or failure of the entrepreneur to adjust production to the demand of the consumers.

Human Action, p. 295; p. 297

No income can be made safe against changes not adequately foreseen.

Human Action, p. 391; p. 394

Seldom does mercantile and industrial wealth maintain itself in one family for more than two or three generations.

Socialism, p. 338

Fortunes invested in capital do not, as the naive economic philosophy of the common man imagines, represent eternal sources of income.

Socialism, p. 338

An eternal capital investment is as non-existent as a secure one. Every capital investment is speculative; its success cannot be foreseen with absolute assurance.

Socialism, p. 339

In capitalist enterprise there is no secure income and no security of wealth.

Socialism, p. 340

Fortunes cannot grow; someone has to increase them.

Socialism, p. 340

If, as is generally the case, the heirs are not equal to the demands which life makes on an entrepreneur, the inherited wealth rapidly vanishes.

Socialism, p. 340

It is untrue that some are poor because others are rich. If an order of society in which incomes were equal replaced the capitalist order, everyone would become poorer.

Socialism, p. 394

The wealth of the well-to-do of an industrial society is both the cause and effect of the masses well-being.

The Ultimate Foundation of Economic Science, p. 113

The masses, in their capacity as consumers, ultimately determine everybody's revenues and wealth.

The Ultimate Foundation of Economic Science, p. 112

WELFARE

The Welfare State is merely a method for transforming the market economy step by step into socialism.

Planning for Freedom, p. 219

The policies advocated by the welfare school remove the incentive to saving on the part of private citizens. On the one hand, the measures directed toward a curtailment of big incomes and fortunes seriously reduce or destroy entirely the wealthier people's power to save. On the other hand, the sums which people with moderate incomes previously contributed to capital accumulation are manipulated in such a way as to channel them into the lines of consumption.

Human Action, p. 841; pp. 844–45

An essential point in the social philosophy of interventionism is the existence of an inexhaustible fund which can be squeezed forever. The whole system of interventionism collapses when this fountain is drained off: The Santa Claus principle liquidates itself.

Human Action, p. 854; p. 858

All almsgiving inevitably tends to pauperize the recipient.

Socialism, p. 422

If the will to be well and efficient is weakened, illness and inability to work is caused.

Socialism, pp. 431–32

The problems of poor relief are problems of the arrangement of consumption, not of the arrangement of production activities. They are as such beyond the frame of a theory of human action which refers only to the provision of the means required for consumption, not to the way in which these means are consumed. Catallactic theory deals with the methods adopted for the charitable support of the destitute only as far as they can possibly affect the supply of labor. It has sometimes happened that the policies applied in poor relief have encouraged unwillingness to work and the idleness of able-bodied adults.

Human Action, p. 600; p. 603

The Welfare State with its methods of easy money, credit expansion and undisguised inflation continually takes bites out of all claims payable in units of the nation's legal tender.

Liberty and Property, p. 25

WESTERN CIVILIZATION

Western civilization is based upon the libertarian principle and all its achievements are the result of the actions of free men.

Economic Freedom and Interventionism, p. 150

The distinctive principle of Western social philosophy is individualism.

Liberty and Property, p. 25

The social system of private property and limited government is the only system that tends to debarbarize all those who have the innate capacity to acquire personal culture.

Liberty and Property, p. 26

The eminence of the Western nations consisted in the fact that they succeeded better in checking the spirit of predatory militarism than the rest of mankind and that they thus brought forth the social institutions required for saving and investment on a broader scale.

Human Action, p. 497; p. 500

The nations of Western Europe brought forth the political and institutional conditions for safeguarding saving and investment on a broader scale, and thus provided the entrepreneurs with the capital needed.

Omnipotent Government, p. 101

The essential characteristic of Western civilization that distinguishes it from the arrested and petrified civilizations of the East was and is its concern for freedom from the state.

The Ultimate Foundation of Economic Science, p. 98

All the marvelous achievements of Western civilization are fruits grown on the tree of liberty.

The Theory of Money and Credit, p. 454

WORK

The only means of inducing a man to work more and better is to offer him a higher reward. It is vain to bait him with the joy of labor. When the dictators of Soviet Russia, Nazi Germany, and Fascist Italy tried to assign to the joy of labor a definite function in their system of production, they saw their expectations blighted.

Human Action, p. 589; p. 592

The hired man does not owe the employer gratitude; he owes him a definite quantity of work of a definite kind and quality.

Human Action, p. 629; p. 634

The toiler looks at his work as a means for the attainment of an end sought, and the progress of his work delights him as an approach toward his goal. His joy is a foretaste of the satisfaction conveyed by the mediate gratification. In the frame of social cooperation this joy manifests itself in the contentment of being capable of holding one's ground in the social organism and of rendering services which one's fellow men appreciates either buying the product or in remunerating the labor expended. The worker rejoices because he gets self-respect and the consciousness of supporting himself and his family and not being dependent on other people's mercy.

Human Action, p. 586; p. 589

WORKERS

Workers and consumers are, of course, identical.

On the Manipulation of Money and Credit, p. 179

The laborer is an entrepreneur in so far as his wages are determined by the price the market allows for the kind of work he can perform. This price varies according to the change in conditions in the same way in which the price of every other factor of production varies.

Human Action, p. 255; p. 254

The American worker is badly mistaken when he believes that his high standard of living is due to his own excellence.

Planning for Freedom, p. 136

The improvement of well-being brought about by capitalism made it possible for the common man to save and thus to become in a modest way himself a capitalist.

Planning for Freedom, p. 160

Everybody is eager to charge for his services and accomplishments as much as the traffic can bear. In this regard there is no difference between the workers, whether unionized or not, the ministers and teachers on the one hand and the entrepreneurs on the other hand. Neither of them has the right to talk as if he were Francis d'Assisi.

Planning for Freedom, p. 145

A great part of the capital at work in American enterprises is owned by the workers themselves and by other people with modest means.

Economic Policy, p. 86

In the market economy the worker sells his services as other people sell their commodities. The employer is not the employee's lord. He is simply the buyer of services which he must purchase at their market price.

Human Action, p. 629; pp. 633–34

WORKING CONDITIONS

It is not labor legislation and labor-union pressure that have shortened hours of work and withdrawn married women and children from the factories; it is capitalism, which has made the wage earner so prosperous that he is able to buy more leisure time for himself and his dependents. The nineteenth century's labor legislation by and large achieved nothing more than to provide a legal ratification for changes which the interplay of market factors had brought about previously.

Human Action, p. 612; pp. 616–17

YOUTH

It has always been the task of the new generation to provoke changes.

Bureaucracy, p. 95

New generations grow up with clear eyes and open minds. And they will approach things from a disinterested, unprejudiced standpoint, they will weigh and examine, will think and act with forethought.

Socialism, p. 13

It is evident that youth is the first victim of the trend toward bureaucratization. The young men are deprived of any opportunity to shape their own fate. For them there is no chance left. They are in fact "lost generations" for they lack the most precious right of every rising generation, the right to contribute something new to the old inventory of civilization.

Bureaucracy, p. 97

Most men are accessible to new ideas only in their youth. With the progress of age the ability to welcome them diminishes, and the knowledge acquired earlier turns into dogma.

Epistemological Problems of Economics, p. 184

BIBLIOGRAPHY

The Anti-Capitalistic Mentality (Spring Mills, Pa.: Libertarian Press, [1956] 1972).

Austrian Economics: An Anthology (Irvington-on-Hudson, N.Y.: Foundation for Economic Education, 1996) edited by Bettina Bien Greaves.

Bureaucracy (New Rochelle, N.Y.: Arlington House, [1944] 1969).

A Critique of Interventionism (New Rochelle, N.Y.: Arlington House Publishers, [1929] 1977).

Defense, Controls, and Inflation (Chicago, Ill.: University of Chicago Press, 1952) edited by Aaron Director.

Economic Calculation in the Socialist Commonwealth (Auburn, Ala.: Ludwig von Mises Institute, [1920] 1990).

Economic Freedom and Interventionism (Irvington-on-Hudson, N.Y.: Foundation for Economic Education, 1990).

Economic Policy: Thoughts for Today and Tomorrow (Chicago, Ill.: Regnery Gateway, 1979).

Epistemological Problems of Economics (New York., N.Y.: New York University Press, [1933] 1981).

The Historical Setting of the Austrian School (Auburn, Ala.: Ludwig von Mises Institute, [1969] 1984).

Human Action: A Treatise on Economics, 1st ed. (Auburn, Ala.: Ludwig von Mises Institute, [1949] 1999, 3rd revised ed. (Chicago, Ill.: Henry Regnery, 1966). (First page number to the 1st edition, second page number to the 3rd edition.)

Interventionism: An Economic Analysis (Irvington-on-Hudson, N.Y.: Foundation for Economic Education, [1940] 1998).

Liberalism: In the Classical Tradition. (Irvington-on-Hudson, N.Y.: Foundation for Economic Education, [1927] 1985).

Liberty and Property (Auburn, Ala.: Ludwig von Mises Institute, [1958] 1988).

On the Manipulation of Money and Credit (Dobbs Ferry, N.Y.: Free Market Books, [1923-46] 1978) edited by Bettina Bien and Percy L. Greaves.

Money, Method, and the Market Process: Essays by Ludwig von Mises (Norwell, Mass.: Kluwer Academic Press, 1990) edited by Richard M. Ebeling.

Nation, State, and Economy: Contributions to the Politics and History of our Time (New York, N.Y.: New York University Press, [1919] 1983).

Ludwig von Mises, Notes and Recollections (South Holland, Ill.: Libertarian Press, [1940] 1978).

Omnipotent Government: The Rise of the Total State and Total War (Spring Mills, Pa.: Libertarian Press, [1944] 1985).

Planned Chaos (Irvington-on-Hudson, N.Y.: Foundation for Economic Education, [1947] 1977).

Planning for Freedom, and Sixteen Other Essays and Addresses (South Holland, Ill.: Libertarian Press), 1980.

Socialism: An Economic and Sociological Analysis (Indianapolis, Ind.: Liberty Press\Liberty Classics, [1922] 1979).

Theory and History (Auburn, Ala.: Ludwig von Mises Institute, [1957] 1985).

The Theory of Money and Credit (Indianapolis, Ind.: Liberty Press\Liberty Classics, [1912] 1981).

The Ultimate Foundation of Economic Science: An Essay on Method (Kansas City, Mo.: Sheed Andrews and McMeel, [1962] 1977).

www.ingramcontent.com/pod-product-compliance
Lightning Source LLC
Chambersburg PA
CBHW082129290526
45794CB00008B/2977